The Prince of Point Lookout

Life, Love and Learning at School of the Ozarks

by
Larry Dablemont

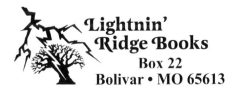

Lightnin' Ridge Books
Box 22
Bolivar • MO 65613

The Prince of Point Lookout
Life, Love and Learning at School of the Ozarks

Copyright 2015 by Larry Dablemont

Published by
Lightnin' Ridge Books

Editor
Sondra Gray

Design and Layout
Ashley Wilson

All rights reserved. No part of this book may be reproduced or transmitted in any form, or by any means, electronic or mechanical, including photocopy, recording, or any other information storage and retrieval system, without the written permission of the author.

**Lighnin' Ridge Books
Box 22, Bolivar, MO 65613**

ISBN: 978-0-9830120-6-1

Library of Congress Control Number: 20-15903403

Table of Contents

1. NO PLANS, NO FUTURE 1
2. ON THE WAITING LIST 7
3. OFF TO COLLEGE 14
4. THE FIRST WEEK 21
5. THE GIRL IN THE T-BIRD 32
6. MEETING DR. CLARK 36
7. McWORTHLESS 43
8. IN TROUBLE EARLY 50
9. HAY-HAULERS 55
10. DR. NIGHTINGALE 62
11. NETTIE MARIE'S BASS 71
12. JAY JOHNSON 81
13. THE RAFFLE 86
14. JULIA, CECIL AND MERVIN 108
15. THE DUCK HUNT 117
16. TRANSPORTATION 130
17. DARRELL HAMBY 136
18. HUSTLERS 143
19. FOREIGNERS 149
20. THE BIG BASS 154
21. PETER ENGLER & STEVE MILLER 164
22. LANE DAVIS 176
23. TOWNSEND GODSEY 181
24. REUBEN 186
25. FINDING FAITH 198
26. CHARLENE & GLORIA JEAN 205
27. YEARS THAT PASSED TOO FAST 215

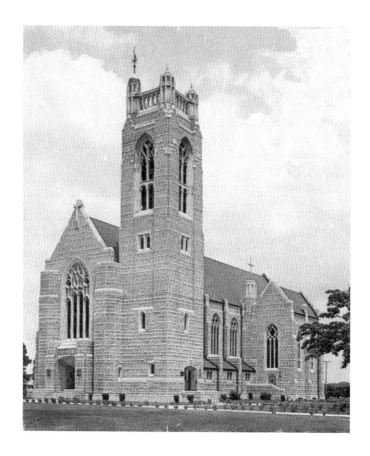

Introduction

The Prince of Point Lookout!

That title sounds a little conceited doesn't it? Well, here's the story behind it.

School of the Ozarks didn't have many no-accounts going to school there, but it had one. I'll just call him Mark McWorthless through this whole book, so he won't try to sue me for pointing out who he was.

Once he made the comment that if Dr. Clark, the school

president, was the King of Point Lookout, I must be the Prince, since I worked for him and spoke often of my admiration for him. McWorthless started calling me the 'Prince of Point Lookout' every time our paths crossed, because he knew how much it riled me. He wasn't highly thought of, and in all the time I was there, he was the only student who used that title for me.

I'll write all about Mark McWorthless at one point in this book, but I will concentrate more on the most wonderful bunch of people I ever knew… professors and administrators and work supervisors and students who helped me mature and gain confidence in myself in the two years I was there.

You won't find much criticism in this book of the School of the Ozarks I knew. Whatever praise you have heard over the years about this place where very poor kids like me could get an education and learn how to be successful in life… it was all true.

God gave me those two years as a blessing, and I was never able to return anything to the school during the time I was trying to make a living as a free-lance writer and raise a family. But with this book, I hope to give back enough to perhaps finance the education of at least one young man today or tomorrow who is a little like I was back then. And that is a big part of its purpose.

I hope this book gives you some laughs, some insight and some inspiration, and a really good look at a great place we called School of the Ozarks.

Larry Dablemont

On graduation day at Houston High School, at the age of 17, I was sure I would never again graduate from anything. I was the first of my grandfather's descendants to get a high school education and I was looking forward to joining the army or finding a good job somewhere, maybe at the local shoe factory. And I had never heard of a place called School of the Ozarks.

Chapter I

NO PLANS, NO FUTURE

"School of the Ozarks!" he said. Houston High School guidance counselor, Cloyce Gerdes, sat across from me at his desk and repeated it. "School of the Ozarks... ever hear of it?

"Mr. Gerdes," I answered, "I've been goin' to school all my doggone life, ain't I done enough?"

He grinned at me, and then the principal of the high school walked in. Mrs. Grace Coats had been a teacher when my dad was a high school student. Now she was the principal, and she wasn't anyone to mess with. She just always had a stern look on her face, and I couldn't figure out why. I was always trying to make her laugh, figuring that no matter what I did, she wouldn't kick me out of school if she was happy. Since that time I had been kicked out of school in the fifth grade, I had stayed out of any serious trouble.

"We are all a little disappointed in you, young man." She told me, "Out of 132 students you are 64th. Why have you been so content with being average over the last four years?"

"There ain't nothin' wrong with being average is there?" I asked her. "I had to work after school all these years you know at my dad's pool hall, and I never did flunk nothin'. I am the first Dablemont I ever heard of who graduated high school... if I actually do."

Believe it or not I saw Mrs. Coats smile, and Mr. Gerdes shook his head while he listened, grinning just a little. Then the stern looks came back.

Mrs. Coats looked down at the papers in her hand. "You placed in the top five on this test!" The test she was talking about was something that had the word 'Ohio' in it. I wasn't real sure where Ohio was back then.

We had to take the test one day before graduation, and it took darn near all day to complete it. I had hurried through it so that if I got finished early, my cousin Dwain and I could get down to the Piney and fish for goggle-eye. They had told me I did well on it, but I knew the only way I could have done good on that test is if Mary Lou Troutman or Ross Duff's paper or one of the other really intelligent kids in my class got mixed up with mine somehow. I was tempted to ask if any really smart kid's score was down toward the bottom, which would explain what had happened.

Sometimes I think when a kid's grandmother is a wonderful woman who prays for him all the time, the Good Lord takes a hand in things and makes strange things happen. You can call those strange things miracles I suppose. For me to wind up on the top rung of any kind of scholastic test would have to be the result of direct divine intervention and a miracle along the lines of Lazarus being raised from the dead.

Mrs. Coats was back to her stern look, shaking those papers in front of me. "Do you realize that you had the intelligence to do very well in school, and you squandered that opportunity? You could have done so much better than to be 64th out of a class of 132," she said. "If you would have lived up to your potential, if you had just worked at it… you could have received scholarships!"

On that day in April or May, I can't remember which, I had only been 17 years old for about four months. When it came to life on the river, or running a pool hall, or making enough money to buy my own clothes, I was a grown man. When it came to social life or an awareness of the things of the world, I was still about 13 years old. I knew nothing about nothing, and I was so immature I didn't even know what a scholarship was. One of my teachers told me I needed to join the army, and I was seriously considering becoming a marine. For a kid like me, from a family so poor you never really had enough money to buy essentials; there was no hope of college, no talk of it. Kids like me were just proud to get a high school diploma.

I decided it was time to get serious, and I nearly teared up. I remember what I told her. "Mrs. Coats," I said, "I can outrun any kid in the doggone high school, but I couldn't go out for track or football, 'cause after school I got to work at my dad and grandpa's pool hall. I ain't got but a half dozen friends, and some of them is my cousins. I got no use for them kids here that call me 'the pool hall kid'. The reason I work at the pool hall is cause my grandpa is too old to work all day, and I got to go there after school so my dad can get home from the shoe factory and rest awhile before he comes in to spell me. I can paddle a johnboat from one side all day on Saturday when I guide fishermen down the Piney. I can beat most grown men in a game of snooker and I go to church on Sundays on account of, I can't whip my dad. I don't cuss and I don't smoke and I don't drink for that same reason. There's things I can do and things I can't and one of the things I can't is understand what those books are talking about that the teachers want me to know. I had that geometry stuff for six months and I still ain't got no idea what it means. Mrs. Gilliam hates me and so does Mrs. Hambacker and the only teacher who ever told me I was a good student, got fired the week afterward. The last thing I ever thought about was college, and I sure ain't got the money to go to one, even if they'd have me."

It was quite a speech for someone as introverted as I was, and it was quiet for a long, long time, as Mrs. Coats just stared at me, something like my mom did before she'd whack me with something. Then she turned to Mr. Gerdes and said, "Let's see if we can get him into School of the Ozarks." He nodded his head and she walked out and I never saw her again. Looking back on it, I wish I could have hugged that lady. Today, I wish I could just see her and Mr. Gerdes again so I could thank them.

Mr. Gerdes told me to sit down at a table and he handed me a form applying for entrance at School of the Ozarks. It looked complicated, and I told him so. He said he'd help me. We had it done in 30 minutes and I headed for home, anxious to go fishing that evening with cousin Dwain. What a waste of time that was, I told myself.

I don't remember how I found out that I had been refused admission to School of the Ozarks College. I think maybe Mr. Gerdes told me. I knew it would happen though. I never did get any breaks. Colleges don't want normal kids, they want special ones, the ones who are good looking and can play a piano and read Shakespeare. I told my dad I was awful glad I wasn't going to have to go, but he was awful disappointed. He said he hoped I could get the education he would have liked to have had, but never got the opportunity. He said he wanted me to do better than he had done. But I told him I would be happy just to live there in Houston and fish and hunt ducks on the Big Piney with him, maybe someday run a big johnboat building enterprise and a float-fishing business.

The day after graduation, I went down to an auto body shop in the hollow east of the courthouse and asked the owner if he could use a good body man, since my uncles were all body men and they had taught me quite a bit. He said he would hire me for a dollar and a quarter an hour, and have me start out sanding cars and taking off parts. I remember how grungy I was the first day after work, my fingers bleeding from sanding cars much of the day. All of a sudden, life didn't seem so good. I didn't have any money, I didn't have a girlfriend, I didn't have a car, I didn't have much of a job... I didn't have much of a future. But my Grandma McNew was still praying.

I didn't remember Mr. Gerdes telling me that while School of the Ozarks College had turned me down, they had put me on a waiting list. That waiting list didn't mean much. Every time I had ever been on a waiting list I had just kept waiting and waiting for nothing. Sharon Bennett had put me on a waiting list of sorts, telling me that someday she might consider being my girlfriend. That was in the second grade and I waited all through high school while she dated the quarterback and later married him. I had been on Donna Hines' waiting list, Lou Gladden's waiting list and Ruthie Gobble's waiting list, all for nothing. Now I was on School of the Ozarks' waiting list. Big deal!

No, let me rephrase that... it is hard to study when you would rather do just about anything else!

Chapter 2

ON THE WAITING LIST

I worked at the body shop for three days. It was hard, awful work. My mom had to change my sheets every morning because there was blood on them from my bleeding fingers. The sanding took my fingerprints away, and they oozed blood. I could have robbed the bank, and they could have never caught me because I had no fingerprints.

But that Friday evening I got almost thirty-five dollars in wages, and I borrowed Dad's car, a 1959 Rambler, and went to the movies with my cousin Butch. We put fifty cents' worth of gas in the car and drove around awhile after the movie looking for girls, but we didn't find any in the time allowed by only fifty cents worth of gas. I was home before midnight and I knew that Dad and I had to put a new roof on the house really early in the morning before it got hot.

Dad had got a real bargain on shingles, and he knew how to put them on. He showed me how you had to start at the top and work down, and overlap them so the roof wouldn't leak. I was surprised he knew how to do that. By ten in the morning, we were almost finished, since our house wasn't that big. I was up there nailing away when Mom came out and said I had a telephone call and it wasn't anyone she knew. I almost told her to tell him to call back later, but then I got to thinking it might be someone from the Marine Corps wanting to offer me a job as a corporal or something, so I climbed down the ladder.

When I picked up the phone, the conversation went something like this.

"Hello."

"Hello sir, is this Larry Dablemont?"

"Yep, that's me."

"Well Mr. Dablemont, (nobody ever called me Mr. Dablemont before... it had to be the Marines) this is David Timmons. I am the registrar at School of the Ozarks College. You'll remember that we had you on our waiting list for incoming freshmen, and this past week we had five incoming freshmen drop out, and you were fifth on our list so we have a place for you if you would like to accept it."

I think about it often. In the freshman class at School of the Ozarks College, probably around 200 kids, I was the very last one taken! The very last one!

I don't have any idea what was said after I quit dancing around the room that day, but I told Mr. Timmons I would be there in a couple of hours. He laughed and said I could come whenever I wanted, but I didn't have to be there until about five o'clock on Sunday evening. He said to report to a Mrs. Swenty at Foster Hall. I remember that he said it was awfully good to hear someone that happy about coming to his school, and he said to be in his office no later than 9 a.m. on Monday morning.

Maybe there hasn't ever been so much joy in our home. My dad had a grin on his face like I have never seen, and my mom was getting all teary-eyed, thinking that I would be home only one more night and then gone forever. My sister Muriel was only about 14 and a freshman in high school. It was a special day for her too, because Muriel was to become one of Houston High School's few four-point valedictorians, and then follow me to School of the Ozarks where she would graduate a four-point valedictorian there.

S of O had no idea what I would be worth to them. Because of me, my sister would be one of their top students someday. My high school grade point was about 2.5, and at S of O, it would only be about 2.2. I was going to a college where no one would remember me much, and I wouldn't be making any great contribution. In fact, if you look back in the yearbooks from 1965 through 1967 you won't even find a picture of me. But Muriel became a VIP at S of O. Over the years, when I tell someone from that time that I went to School of the Ozarks, they invariably say, "Dablemont???? Hey were you any relation to Muriel?"

Mom had one big old black suitcase that looked like it had been used by a mafia member in the 1920's to carry machine guns, but it held everything I owned. On Saturday evening, we went to Forbes Drugstore and bought me some toothpaste and Right Guard deodorant, and then on over to Leavitt's Department Store where I got a new shirt and a new pair of white Levi's.

I was going to pay for them, but Dad wouldn't let me. It was quite a concession for someone who never could understand why I wouldn't just wear a pair of four-dollar overalls to school like kids had worn in his day.

Dad was beaming. He told everyone he came across that I was going to college. Looking back, I wish to gosh it had been him going, when he was 17 years old. I know what he could have accomplished if he had had such an opportunity. In the years after I went to S of O, and the years when eventually both my sisters went, Dad joined up for night classes at the Houston High School and got his G.E.D. He had quit high school as a freshman, so he could work and support himself in St. Louis, on his own at the age of 14. He was smarter than I was, when you get right down to it. He too didn't know much about social things of that day either, but folks admired him, and I felt like there couldn't have been a better dad anywhere.

While we were in college, he got a chance to drive a school bus for the Houston School District, and he quit the shoe factory for good. In his years driving the bus, he became the number one driver, and was always the one they called on to make special trips around to various towns, both day and night. He was a very happy man, and one of the things that made him happiest back then was the fact that his son, the pool hall kid, was going to college.

We went to church that Sunday morning, and in that little congregation of thirty or forty people, filled with friends of my folks and kids my age who had grown to mean a lot to me, there was a lot of excitement. Preacher Morton announced it at the pulpit, and a little 14-year-old girl who was a friend of my sister actually smiled at me and batted her eyes a little. I noticed she had on some make-up and didn't look as young as she had a month or so before.

Tom and Roy Wayne Morton, who were the preacher's nephews, were awfully sad about it. They were both younger than me, by just a year or two, and we did a lot of fishing together over the years, and had lots of fun in church with the various activities they had going for kids. I told them I wouldn't be far away, and I would come home on weekends and we'd go trotlining just like we always had.

My dad, Farrel Dablemont, was elated that I had a chance to go to college. He hadn't even had the opportunity to go to high school. Dad was such an intelligent man, there is no telling where he could have gone with the education School of the Ozarks gave me. He and my grandfather bought a pool hall in Houston, Missouri and I went to work there when I was only eleven and worked there for five years. He kept it a respectable place, and raised me to be the best I could be. I never knew a man I respected more.

After church I visited my grandparents for a short time. They were my mother's folks, Bert and Hilda McNew, and they meant a lot to me. I told them not to worry, I would be coming home a lot on account of, the college didn't want kids staying there on weekends. I just made that up, but they didn't know any better.

Back then, there was no big highway from Springfield to Branson. They were working on it, but you had to go from Houston to Mansfield, down to Ava and over to Branson via a little winding highway which went through Kirbyville and then Forsyth. There was some beautiful scenery, a part of Missouri I had never seen before. But when you got right down to it, I hadn't seen much of anything in Missouri but Texas County.

Finally, after about two hours, there it was… the campus of School of the Ozarks College. My gosh it was big…and beautiful. There was well-mowed green grass, and flowers everywhere. Right in the center of the place there was a gosh awful huge rock chapel with a bell tower reaching up toward heaven. When we pulled up in front of Foster Hall Dormitory, it started chiming, just like it was heralding my arrival. There was a minute or so of some kind of ringing, and then four chimes. It was four o'clock on Sunday evening, June 9, 1965. At that moment, a new life began for me. Even today, after all those years, I still remember the feeling I had right then, seeing it for the first time. And it was one of the most wonderful feelings I had ever felt.

Chapter 3

OFF TO COLLEGE

I still had about 25 dollars left of the wages I had made during the week at the body shop. I tried to call my boss there before I left, to thank him for giving me a job, and to tell him why I was leaving. Dad told me that he would go by on Monday and tell him all that for me.

Dad and Mom and my younger sisters and I went all around the campus that Sunday afternoon and they agreed it was one of the prettiest places they had ever seen. That cathedral was spectacular. And there was a walkway at the west edge, center of the campus, that led down to a high lookout point on a rock bluff with an overview of the whole valley of Lake Taneycomo way down below, and from it you could see as far as Table Rock Lake miles to the southwest. In that time, there was little development in that beautiful valley, and you could see little but forest and fields. One of those fields was owned by the School and later in the summer I would be bucking bales and hauling hay over there, with a crew of farm boys whom I would get to know well.

We met the dorm mother, Mrs. Swenty, a middle-aged redheaded lady that was very pretty and sweet-natured, and she answered a lot of questions for Mom. The room they gave me was on the second floor of Foster Hall. It was awfully small, and Mrs. Swenty told me all about my roommate, who would be coming back later that evening. I stowed all my stuff in drawers, and a little closet, and took a look at the bunk I would be sleeping on. It looked just as comfortable as the one I had at home.

Foster Hall was the oldest dormitory on campus. It was the place where most incoming freshmen landed. They had a bigger dormitory, Smith Hall, which was much newer, with bigger rooms and a nicer restroom and showers. I never did see much of it, because Foster Hall would be my residence for the next two full years, even through the summer.

There was a big pay phone on the first floor, as I remember, and before he left, Dad gave me some dimes, in case I had to call him to come and get me. I told him I would give the dimes back to him someday, because I was there to stay. Neither of us were real confident in that.

When my folks drove away a couple of hours later, I felt more alone and lonely than I had ever felt. Back in Houston I knew everyone, from the merchants up and down Main Street to the old timers in the pool hall, and every kid within three years of my age. Now suddenly, there were hundreds of young men and women everywhere, and I didn't know a soul. There wasn't a human being anywhere who knew who I was. And it felt as if there wasn't a soul anywhere who gave a darn who I was. I walked around a while, noticing there was a lot of building going on. School of the Ozarks was in earlier years, a high school for poor Ozarks' kids from very strapped families, kids who likely would have dropped out of school where they lived.

The summer I got there, they still had remnants of two

high school classes, and a small group of high school students. Within a couple of years when all of them had graduated, the high school was terminated and School of the Ozarks became known as a fully accredited four-year liberal arts college. But liberal it wasn't... thank goodness. It was a place where common values remained, and common sense prevailed.

That evening a very clean cut, well dressed group of girls and boys were sitting on the porch in front of Foster Hall as the sun set and the bells rang in the cathedral, marking the end of the Sunday evening church service. Twin brothers by the last name of Wilson were playing guitars and singing, and some of the kids sitting around were singing with them. I thought to myself, "Gosh these are bona fide college kids, what the heck am I doing here?"

I walked into the recreation room, where there was a T.V. and a couple of young men sprawled out on a couch watching T.V. I wished Mom and Dad hadn't left so early; I just wanted to go home.

I felt someone walk up behind me and an arm went around my shoulder. I looked to my right and there stood Mrs. Swenty, with a big smile on her face and a hug for me.

"It isn't easy the first few nights and days, but you'll make it," she said still smiling. "I will be in my residence here next to the office any time you need me, and I am always ready to talk with any of my boys here... that includes you."

I told her that I was worried about where to go and what to do the next day. I felt really out of place. "I'll help you with all that until you get settled," she said. "That's my job. You come back down here in the morning about seven and

I'll get you fixed up for breakfast at the dining hall before you get your I. D. card. Then come back and I'll get you an agenda to follow, and a map to show you how to get where you need to go."

She looked at me for a moment and squeezed my shoulders. "Did you know you are the youngest student in my dorm?" she said, "In two weeks you will feel at home, and know everything there is to know about S of O. Tonight, just go out and introduce yourself and make acquaintances with some of the kids, then get an early shower and get some sleep."

I thanked her and started to walk back out on the porch, where dusk was settling.

My dorm mother Mrs. Swenty, was a sweet lady.

Behind me, Mrs. Swenty called me by my first name. I turned around and she said it again, "Everything will be fine... don't worry." I've got to say, that lady over the next two years was a pillar of strength for every boy in that dorm. I never heard a negative thing said about her. I came to love her, as did many others. Dozens of times I went to her when I was feeling down, talking to her as if she was indeed a mother with about 200 sons. There were some angels at S of O and Mrs. Swenty was one of them.

I went up to my room and sat there feeling as if I had made a big mistake. I didn't know a soul within a hundred miles, and for the first time in my young life, I knew what loneliness was. I shouldn't have been there, I knew. I was the fifth kid on the waiting list and five kids had quit and gone home. There must have been a reason for that. I thought about the sixth kid on that waiting list and wondered if I might have kept him from doing great things with an education he or she would never get. There I was in his place because a couple of test scores got mixed up. If I had known how to call that sixth kid on the waiting list and tell him to come and take my place that evening, I would have.

About that time my roommate came through the door. He was a big fellow with a chiseled face and a strong handshake. I thought to myself that he and I had better get along, 'cause I sure couldn't whip him.

"J. B. King's the name," he said, "glad you are here... I've been here most of the week alone."

Let me go into detail about J.B. He was one of those guys who was gung-ho about everything. He was the kind of fellow a marine sergeant would have loved, because he could do about anything, and like I said, he was enthused. I know that somewhere, J.B. will find and read this book, and so I want to tell you a little about what he became.

Out of college, I heard J.B. became a highway patrolman.

My brother-in-law, who was also a highway patrolman, said they worked only a couple of counties apart, and all you ever heard about J.B. and his work was positive. In time he ran for sheriff up around Ft. Leonard Wood and Rolla, and served in that capacity for some time, working in an area where there were lots of problems because of all the army servicemen. He had a tough job there, because when you assemble that many soldiers, if a small percentage of them are inclined to get drunk and get in fights and that type of thing, you had better be a real lawman.

But I will always remember J.B. for one thing that happened about the third or fourth night I was at S of O. He was just a kid like I was, and he had been there a couple of weeks, undergoing training as a part of the school's student fire department. That group of young men did a good job, and I am sure some of them continued in careers as firefighters. Their supervisors emphasized getting to the fire trucks as quickly as possible when that siren went off, no matter where they were on campus.

One night about ten, with all the lights out and the campus quiet and peaceful outside the dorm window, I had just drifted off to sleep. J.B. was on the top bunk, and I assumed he was asleep too. In a sudden rush, he came out of that bunk as if someone had thrown a rattlesnake in with him, hitting the floor and dressing in the dark in a wild flurry of near panic. I thought something awful must have happened to him. Suddenly he turned on the lights as I sat up, my heartbeat going up around a hundred and fifty, my breath catching as I tried to ask what was wrong. He was standing there completely dressed, looking at his watch. "Forty-eight seconds", he said. "I am going to have to beat that!"

It suddenly dawned on me what had happened. J.B. had decided to see how quickly he could get ready if the fire alarm sounded in the middle of the night. That night, I knew my heart was fairly sound.

Chapter 4

THE FIRST WEEK

I can't remember much about that Monday morning, the first time I saw the dawn at S of O. The bells at the chapel sounded beautiful that morning at 7 a.m.

Mrs. Swenty told me how to find the cafeteria, but all I had to do was follow the stream of young men heading that way.

I never had been too high on eating breakfast at home, because we never had much. Sometimes in high school I'd have a piece of toast and fried baloney. I know that in Italy or France or wherever the heck they invented it, they spell it 'bologna'. In the Ozarks, it has always been spelled, and pronounced, 'baloney'. It has a dual meaning where I came from. It can refer to the meat that everyone made sandwiches out of, a round slice with a red piece of plastic around it that you have to remove. I heard once that baloney is made from scraps of meat, and things like beef tongue. Never mattered to me. When you intended to go fishing or hunting, you could go to the grocery store and get thick-sliced 'baloney' and some 'mannaze' and a loaf of bread and have a very economical and tasty sandwich on some river gravel bar or in the front seat of your pick-up. Whatever it is made of, it is really good when you fry it in the morning and put it on a piece of toast and lay a fried egg on top of it. That's what I had for breakfast quite often, unless we were out of eggs, or baloney or bread.

The cafeteria that morning was a little like the one we had in high school. Several ladies were on the other side of the steaming aluminum tables where there were scrambled eggs and bacon and sausage and even pancakes. A couple of them looked like they had seen their dog run over by a truck before they came to work, but a couple were smiling and laughing and cheerful.

"Ain 't you got no fried baloney?" I asked one of them.

She smiled at me and replied that she would try to have some the next morning. Then she added, "You're new here, aren't you?"

I nodded and she gave me an extra pancake with a parting smile. The whole time I was there, that lady worked in the cafeteria, and she was always happy and smiling, despite all the griping that she had to listen to. I mention this because later in this book I will come back to her in another chapter.

At the table there were young men and women I would come to know very well, and some I would never get acquainted with. There were some like me, who thought it was a great breakfast, and some who complained how awful it was. There were a handful of students who never were satisfied with anything there at School, and if you saw or heard them anywhere it was at church or in the cafeteria, the two places where they griped the most.

All the time I was at S of O, I loved the meals, all of them. The problem was, I couldn't get enough dessert. When I heard some kid talking about how he couldn't stand that slop at the cafeteria, I wondered if he came from some rich family that ate caviar and lobster. I have a feeling

The school cafeteria, a little too small and filled to capacity at mealtimes. I thought the food there was great, but so many students complained that we all thought we had to, just to fit in. Secretly, I never ate better in my life.

that those who complained back then are still complaining today about something. What made me mad was, a couple of them were from foreign countries, no doubt getting everything given to them, taking up places at the School, and opportunities that some Ozark boys would have loved to have had.

After breakfast that morning, I came back to the dorm and took a shower. On each floor there was a big bathroom with four commodes, and four showerheads, no partitions anywhere, and four sinks with mirrors.

I waited in line to take a shower, and shaved just like I really needed to, even though I really didn't, in front of one of the mirrors like the other guys. It isn't something you would find in a college dormitory today, but back then, it worked. Students running around half-naked up and down the halls weren't a problem. Most of us were freshmen, as the upper classmen lived in that newer dormitory known as Smith Hall, where they had a much more modern facility.

Foster Hall was old and rooms were small, bathrooms not at all modernized. This is probably a good place to mention that somewhere after the time I was there, they converted Foster Hall to a woman's dormitory and really fixed it up. My daughter Leah attended S of O from 1997 to 2001, and though this is hard to believe, the room she was given was the same room I had moved into that first night in June of 1965. In 1997 it had become a girls' dorm. By then, the bathrooms had partitions, and the rooms were painted and had new light fixtures and windows. Leah was only there a short time before moving into a big, newer girls' dorm, but for a while she lived in the same room her dad had lived in 32 years before. It seemed unbelievable that could have happened.

At 9 a.m. I was in the registrar's office. I got to meet the man who had called me to tell me I had been accepted at S of O, his name was David Timmons. He was young, maybe not even thirty years old yet. He shook my hand and grinned and asked me if I was still as anxious to go to school as I had been on the previous Saturday afternoon.

If you stop and think about it, my life was changed in such an unusual way. I wonder at times, who was it that sat somewhere behind a desk there and went through applications of hundreds of kids, and put me on a waiting list. Perhaps it was Mr. Timmons, maybe someone whose name I will never know. Obviously I didn't have the kind of grade point a college looks for in its students. Truthfully,

I doubt there were any kids accepted that year that had a high school grade point as low as mine. But I am what I am today, most likely, because Mr. Timmons called me and told me five kids had quit and gone home. I was the very last student accepted for that summer semester, and I doubt that I would be here today if that fifth kid hadn't quit. Viet Nam loomed just ahead, and there's little doubt that if I hadn't gone to S of O, I would have soon joined the army.

I don't labor under some misguided idea that God thought I was special enough to give me any more attention than any other kid. But I was always aware that my grandmother prayed constantly for me. My mother's mother was an angel. Because my Mom had to work so much, I spent a lot of my time at my Grandpa and Grandma McNew's farm as a small boy. On weekends, I would stay there with some of my cousins, and I would hear her prayers often. I think she had a good connection with the Great Creator, and whatever anyone thinks, I know that a grandmother's prayers go a long way to making life better for their grandkids.

As a newcomer, I had to catch up. Most students had been at the School for two weeks, had assigned jobs and had about 40 to 60 hours of work credit. You were given a job, and you worked four hours a day, then went to school the other half of the day. There weren't many jobs left unassigned.

I had to sit down in Mr. Timmons' office and fill out a form telling all about myself, and listing the kinds of part-time and summer jobs I had held back in Houston.

And this is where I get to the other definition of the word, 'baloney'. My days working as a boy in my dad's pool hall had taught me the other definition of it. Baloney can mean a mixed concoction of tall stories, which are almost true

This is one side of a folding postcard I found at S of O the first month I was there, and the other side shows the letter I sent home to my grandmother. There are at least four lies in the first paragraph!!!

Dear Grandma & Grandpa,

Boy have I been busy. I like my classes and I'm spending a lot of time on them so I'll make good grades. My job here is easy and there's lots to do so I haven't gotten too homesick yet.

I hope you like these pictures. They're just a few of the buildings here. Isn't the church pretty. I want you and Grandpa to come up here sometime with Mom and dad. I won't be home this weekend, but I will be home the next. I'll be by to see you then.

How's everyone back home. I wrote Butch a letter, but he hasn't wrote back. Is he going to go to school next year? He should come down here. This is a 4 year college now. He could get as good an education here as anywhere, if he don't mind working for it. That way he wouldn't have to pay back any loans.

Tell everyone I said Hi, and I'll see you in about a week.

Love,
Larry

things remembered and recalled without a certain accuracy that would be needed in a court of law, the ability to skirt lying completely without telling the absolute truth about something. I applied a certain amount of baloney to the account of jobs I had held down.

The first thing I listed was manager of a pool hall, and weekend hunting and fishing guide. Since I had helped Dad build johnboats, I listed carpentry. Since I had been helping him put shingles on our house the day Mr. Timmons called, I listed roofing as one of my abilities. I had worked in my uncle's body shop on occasions, and I had worked for a short period in the local feed mill. So I listed both. Then I remembered that I had worked on a hay crew, putting up hay in the summer for 1 and ½ cents a bale. I had made some money hunting golf balls at the local golf course, so I said I had worked there too. There are a couple of other things I put down that I figured I should list, but I can't remember them all.

Then I went to meet a teacher who was to be my advisor, and I can't remember much about that. I would get to know him better. His name was Mr. Mottesheard and he had been a member of the Missouri Conservation Commission in younger years. When I met him he was teaching conservation courses at S of O. I was told what courses it would be best to take and where all those classes were held, and when. Then someone gave me a tour of the campus showing me which buildings were which. Everywhere we went there were students working at this job or that. I saw the campus landscaping crew working on putting in some flowerbeds and I wished I could work with them.

That afternoon I reported for my first work assignment, in the laundry, helping to fold and bundle clothes for students. Of course everyone who ever knew about the School knows the various jobs students held down. There was the laundry, where all students' clothes came in to be washed, dried, bundled and returned. There was a cannery, a boiler room, a construction crew and a farm crew. Students worked everywhere, in the commissary, the cafeteria, in the dorms. You were given jobs as freshmen that weren't the most glamorous job. I figure those five students who quit so I could go to school, may have quit because the jobs they drew were not to their liking.

There isn't much they could have assigned me where I wouldn't have been happy. After all, I had worked hard all my life, making my own money to buy clothes and things since I was 14 years old. The laundry was said to be one of the least desirable jobs. Shucks, I liked it. There at the laundry I met a couple of girls that looked at me like I was the quarterback of the football team. They didn't have the slightest idea that back home I was the pool hall kid, the one who got kicked out of school in the fifth grade and could barely pass my geometry class.

I had three classes that summer. One was a beginning religion course, another a freshman English class, and the other was a physical education class, I think. The physical education class gave me the most problem, because it was all about the game of basketball. At Houston, I hadn't even gone to one basketball game, and I didn't know a thing about it. Besides, I was only about four feet and eighteen inches tall. There were guys in that class who had shoulders taller than I was.

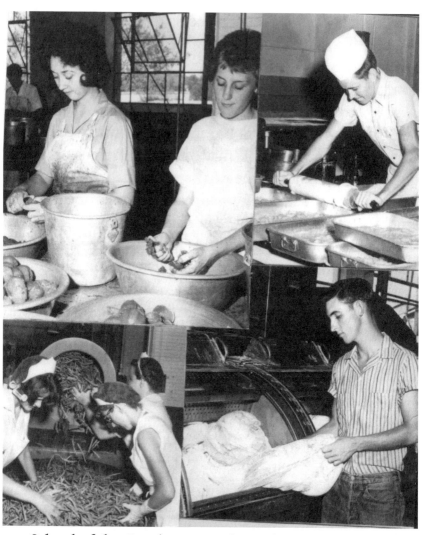

School of the Ozarks was a place where students from around the country could get an education by working at an assigned job on campus for 22 hours a week. Student labor ran the college basically, with supervisors overseeing their work. If you were as poor as I was, School of the Ozarks was the only hope for an education.

Coach Smith didn't like me. He was a nice guy, but really sort of a marine sergeant type and he didn't smile much. He didn't much like the fact that I didn't know the technology of basketball. The idea that you could foul out was foreign to me. I played a little softball and to me a foul just meant you kept batting.

Once he threw a basketball at me as hard as he could and I threw it back at him as hard as I could. Boy that made him mad! I figured that day that I was headed for another C in that class. In time, I got to know Coach Smith better, and I really liked him. He coached the men's basketball team for many years there at S of O. I can't say that he ever really considered me a prospect for the team. And every now and then he would smile.

Chapter 5

THE GIRL IN THE T-BIRD

Because I was behind everyone in work hours accumulated, they told me I would be working at the gate that first full weekend, and wouldn't be expected to go to chapel on Sunday morning. The entrance gate to the School back then was on the southeast side of the campus, and the present entrance, which is used by thousands of visitors each year, with a restaurant and gift shop wasn't even built. There was a little entrance building about six by six, with a roof on it and open windows on each side at the beginning of a tree-lined entrance road. The paved lane on one side went into the school while the road on the other side came out.

I showed up that Saturday morning and found there were two of us there. I think the other guy may have been the fourth student on the waiting list, and like me, he got there a week later than everyone else. His name was Bob Carr, and I found he lived on the same floor as I did in Foster Hall. Bob came from Pierce City or Sarcoxie or some place in that area. Of course when I was 17, I hadn't been hardly anywhere and if it wasn't a town in Texas County then I had no idea where it was.

Bob Carr was the first really good friend I made at S of

O, one of the cheeriest people you could ever imagine. He made anyone who was around him happy, because it seemed he always was. He and I both liked to talk to people and we spent the weekend visiting with folks who were bringing students back to school, or coming to visit. I thoroughly enjoyed it, and wished I could just get a job like that for good. I told Bob as much, and he said he figured the older kids who had been there awhile would fill the good jobs on campus.

Bob Carr

But I didn't care, there were some pretty girls working in that laundry, and unlike what I had experienced in high school, they talked to me just like I was someone special.

But none were as pretty as the young girl who drove through the entrance gate in a black '57 Thunderbird. She had long, straight, glistening black hair, and a big smile showing the whitest teeth I ever saw. Thankfully she was on my side, and I sauntered out there and asked if I could help her with anything.

She shook her head and I couldn't just let her drive off, I had to make a fool of myself.

"Are you coming for a visit, ma'am or are you a student?" I asked. Heck I knew she wasn't a student in that car.

"I'm still in high school," she said. "I live here."

Then she said, "I'll bet you two are new students aren't you?"

"Yep," I answered. "They called me a week ago and told me they needed me down here really bad on account of the overall grade point average here was too high!"

She laughed, so I just kept going. "I really like that car, ma'am. If you ever need someone to shine it up for you, just call me. My name is Larry Dablemont and I live in Room 222 at Foster Hall, and I wax cars for a dollar and a quarter an hour."

With a big smile she said she would remember me. Lord, wouldn't that be nice. I told her just before she drove away that she should contact me soon, as I was expecting to be called before the end of the summer by the St. Louis Cardinals, who wanted me to try out for offensive lineman.

I think she got the joke. I was about 5 foot 7 and weighed about a hundred and forty pounds with a pair of heavy boots on.

As a new car pulled up, I realized that the kid I was, seemed to be gone in only one week. I had said more to that black haired girl than any girl I had ever talked to. It was easy to figure out why. I didn't like the kid I had been in high school, but you couldn't change because everyone had known you since you were a little boy. I had an image to maintain, a kid who didn't like hardly anyone, who had a chip on his shoulder, and maintained a list of people he intended to get even with someday. Back home, I was the pool hall kid and I hated rich people and girls and mean teachers. In one week at School of the Ozarks, I had learned I could just relax and be myself, because all the students there had been raised like me and didn't know a thing about me and my past.

The girl in the Thunderbird was obviously from a rich family, and I had talked to her anyway. It felt good not to be mad at so many people.

Chapter 6

MEETING DR. CLARK

On Sunday afternoon, a real big shot came through. I could tell by looking at him. He had on an expensive suit with a nice tie and was driving a long, light blue, brand new Lincoln Continental.

He stopped and I knew that he would be a good man to make a good impression on, so I asked if I could help him with anything. He laughed and said he thought he pretty much knew where everything was on campus. His accent was pure south, and his voice was loud and strong. He wanted to know how I liked attending the college.

"Well sir," I told him, trying to act a little bit southern myself, opposed to sounding like the hillbilly I was, "I've only just been here a week because I was on a waiting list and several students had to quit before they let me in, but Mister, this is one neat place. It's just beautiful, and in the evening I look out across that river valley from the big old high rock point and wonder if heaven ain't somethin' like this. I only got three classes and the meals here are near about the best I have ever eaten."

He laughed heartily, and asked me if there wasn't something about it I didn't like. "I understand some of the students here complain about a few things," he said.

"Not yet," I told him, and then I let a little bit of that baloney I was born with come through. "Next week though, if I have the time I'm going to go around and look for some things I don't like."

The guy laughed again, and we talked a little more until another car pulled in behind him. I really liked him, and that southern accent was great.

I asked Bob Carr if he knew who the man was, and he didn't. "He sure never went to school here though," Bob said. "That car means he's somebody important. I wouldn't doubt if he doesn't make ten or fifteen thousand dollars a year."

It was nice to have made a friend, and all through my two years at S of O, Bob and I were good friends. While there, we decided to go duck hunting one winter weekend, and the story of that adventure will come later. Bob was an art major, if I remember right, and a good artist even as a freshman at S of O.

I got up early on Monday morning and went to religion class, taught by Doctor Stone. Doc Stone was someone who no doubt knew the Bible, and he taught me a lot about the Bible too, and the people of the Old Testament: who they were and how they lived. I had heard all the Bible stories a million times and thought there was nothing more to hear. Dr. Stone knew things about the Bible that were amazing. He was a short man and fairly heavy, very effeminate and downright soft-looking. He spoke so distinctly and correctly it sounded like he was trying to work at making himself sound a certain way, and there was just a hint of an English accent in him. Later I had a New Testament course he taught, and both courses were very interesting. It all opened my eyes to the Bible as I had never seen it, made me want to know more, especially about those people in the Old Testament.

When I went to the University of Missouri a couple of years later I only had two courses that didn't transfer. Those were Dr. Stone's two classes on the Bible. It seems strange to me. Those classes taught me a great deal and peaked my interest in something I had little interest in before, and yet MU thought they were useless in educating a student. It was only a year or so before the publishing of this book that Missouri University decided to start honoring pagan and wiccan holidays on campus. And yet, my courses on the Bible were of no consequence to them!

When my classes ended that first day, I headed over to the laundry to work a couple of hours folding and packaging clean laundry belonging to the students. Mostly girls worked there, and I thought if I was really lucky I could keep that job for a long time. But I hadn't been there for long until one of the supervisors came along with a note that sunk my spirits right to the depths of despair.

It said to come immediately to the office of the President, and it gave the name of his secretary to report to. That was it.

I was done for. I had been there seven and a half days and they had already decided to kick me out for some little old thing I didn't even know I had done.

The people at the laundry told me how to find the College President's office. They didn't say, "See you later." I figure they knew I was history.

On the way over, I tried to remember what I might have done. I hadn't got into it with anyone, and I hadn't missed a class or been late to work. I had snuck out of the kitchen with an extra cinnamon roll on Saturday morning, convincing the nice lady who served food that my roommate was sick and needed it for sustenance. I guess that had to be it, I thought. Then I got to thinking about how much I had stretched the truth on that form I had filled out detailing my work experience.

I figured I'd throw myself on the mercy of that presidential fellow and promise to do better if he'd let me stay.

His secretary just had me sit down and wait. She smiled at me and asked me if I was nervous. She said I looked like I had lost my best friend. I told her I had just made one friend and if I was going to be kicked out, I certainly had lost my best friend.

She laughed out loud, and got up from her desk and walked around before me. She assured me I wasn't there to be sent home, and she peeked into the President's office to tell him I was waiting. It was as if a giant weight had been lifted from my body. Her name was Jan Hoynacki, and I got to know her better over the two years I was there. She was a fixture on the S of O campus, and the President's right hand lady.

I heard his booming southern voice before I saw him, but when he walked out of that office, you could have knocked me over with a wind-blown pickle seed.

It was him, the guy in the big Lincoln Continental and the suit. I stood up and he shook my hand with that big smile of his. "Lahry," he said with that Georgia accent, "It is nice to see you again."

I went in his office and he bade me sit down in a big chair across from his desk. "Have you had a chance to find anything you don't like yet, young man," he laughed. I just gulped and shook my head. I felt like a fool, remembering how I talked his leg off up at that gate.

I was sitting there in the plush office of the college president in a t-shirt, old blue jeans and tennis shoes.

I was wondering what in the heck did he want me for?

Dr. M. Graham Clark was a pretty good-sized man, probably about 6 foot tall and 200 pounds. His hands were large and his handshake was firm. His hair was thin and graying, but he didn't look any older than 50 to me. He talked loud, and had that Georgia accent, coming across very sure of himself... confident... in charge.

"I surely did enjoy talking with you the other day young man," he told me as he sat down behind his desk. "When I came in this morning I had your information brought to my office." He shuffled through the papers before him and we talked a bit about the little Ozark town I hailed from, and some other small talk.

He kept grinning the whole time he and I talked, like he knew something funny he was going to tell me. Then finally he got to it. "Lahry," he said, (the name Larry sounds like Lah-ree in Georgia.) "I have looked through your work experience, and what you have listed as jobs you held, and I have come to the conclusion that either you have done more kinds of work than any student who ever came here, or you are the doggonedest liar the School of the Ozarks has ever enrolled!" It would have worried me if he hadn't of laughed heartily after he said it.

I never actually looked at baloney as outright lying, but it was awful close at times. I gulped and said something about how being really, really, poor made it necessary to find a lot of different ways to make money.

Dr. Clark then started telling me about his boyhood, and how he understood what being poor was all about. In no time at all, I wasn't afraid of him anymore, and began to

The fellow in the Lincoln Continental I met at the entrance gate was Dr. Montague Graham Clark (back), President of the School, shown here with President Emeritus Robert M. Good. He turned out to be a great boss, and a great friend.

relax. You couldn't help but like him, that strong voice and the southern accent, and that air of confidence. He made me feel like I was really someone he was interested in, that I was important.

"Well, I know you have lots to do, young man so I will get to the reason I had you called in here," he said.

"There are a lot of student jobs here on campus, and I have four young women and two young men who work at my home. I hated to see one of those young men graduate this past spring, but I know he will go on to do great things with his life, so I am very happy about that. But I am needing someone to take his place, and I thought you, with all your experience, (and that's when he started grinning real big again) might like to take over his job."

I had no idea what that job might entail, but I wasn't about to say 'no'. We shook hands on it! I was sure going to miss those girls at the laundry.

Chapter 7

McWORTHLESS

Working for Dr. Clark was wonderful, but when other young men were out doing construction work, and I drove by them in his big Lincoln Continental, after taking him to the airport, it caused some resentment. Mark McWorthless was a sophomore who was full of bitterness for some reason, and he really hated me.

When I had to stop the car once as he and a student construction crew were working on some project without a supervisor present, he exclaimed in a loud voice, "Lookie here fellows, it's the King's chariot. And there's the Prince of Point Lookout driving it!" It got a big laugh of course, and it could have been forgotten right then.

But McWorthless made it a point to rile me every chance he could. It was as if he was trying to pick a fight with me at every opportunity. He wasn't much bigger than me, and I always felt that if I got mad enough I could give him a good tussle. But truthfully, I hated fighting and I just avoided violence as much as I could. As a kid in high school, I didn't fight with anyone, and in order to do something violent, I had to become so enraged it took away my ability to think and reason. That rage resulted in the hatred that had made me compile a list of people I intended to find some day and seek revenge upon. There is nothing healthy about that, nothing good in hatred, as it can consume and destroy you. Still, I wanted more than anything to find a way to throttle that kid!

The closest we came to a fight was the Sunday evening during the first summer I was there, when I was on my way to a chapel service. If you were on campus, your attendance at Sunday morning and Sunday evening church service was required, and if you were caught skipping those services often, you could be expelled from school. Truthfully, I didn't much care about going. I would just sit in the back and snooze a little on occasion and get out in a hurry when it was over. But back in Houston, I had been going to church regularly with my family, to a small Freewill Baptist church where the preacher had tricked me into coming up to the alter at the age of 13 to be "saved" as he put it.

Truthfully, I had no idea what I was doing at the time, the old fire-and-brimstone country preacher told me that in doing so I was saved from the fires of hell, and born again. Surprisingly, I didn't feel one bit different than I had when I was sitting on the back row, about half asleep.

I was baptized in the Big Piney River and that was that. If the preacher figured I was saved, then I wasn't going to worry about it. But when you are seventeen years old and you don't understand hardly anything going on in the world you don't really understand what Christianity is. Back then I remember praying that God would allow one school bully to run off the road in his car and be killed so it would spare the kids he bullied from having to endure him. God refused my prayers of that sort, and surprisingly that school bully became a good man many years later. I guess God had a way of seeing value in people I thought was worthless.

That evening, McWorthless and a couple of his buddies were sitting on the wall where the chapel steps were, and as I walked up, he declared, "Hey Dablemont, are you gonna' get saved tonight?"

I really bristled at that. I told him I was already saved and that the way I saw it, God would probably be sending him to hell soon, as he had no good purpose in life. I said something to the effect that if God didn't snuff him out soon, I might wait 'til after I got out of school, and go back and find him and do that job myself when he least expected it. He got really mad, and so did I. Here I was in front of the Chapel, behaving as if I had no more idea about what God was than he did. My anger rose to a point I began to get loud and I have no idea who it was that came along and broke it all up and told us to shut up and get inside. Then I sat there steaming, listening to that beautiful organ playing "Amazing Grace". You might think that in such a situation I would have asked God to forgive me for being such a poor example. But I didn't. I was sitting there thinking of what I could do to get revenge!

McWorthless was actually no more worthless than I was, but the two of us did a lot of sparring for the next few months. Once when I was crossing campus with a couple of bags of groceries from the cafeteria for the Clark household, he came up beside me and grabbed a banana and ate it, another challenge to me. Again, we came awfully close to a fight right there in the middle of the campus, a fight which would likely have gotten both of us kicked out of school. I told him that I would let Dr. Clark know how much he liked bananas, and you could see the sudden realization on his face that I had him in a rather precarious situation. He recovered quickly however, remarking that the King's little Prince would certainly have to seek his help.

That fall there were flag football teams put together for intramural games, and I joined up, having never played football, and not really knowing much about the game. Of course I was given a spot on the defensive line, and who do you suppose lined up across from me? McWorthless! On the first play he pushed me about 20 yards backwards and really enjoyed it when I went down on my rear. You could hear him laughing as he walked away. It came to me then that I wasn't a football player and I walked off the field and quit the team after only one play, never to try that again.

I got even the following spring when we were playing in an intramural softball game and I was running from first to second. McWorthless was fielding a ground ball right in line with second base and in a defenseless position, so I just lowered my shoulder and ran over him. It flattened him and addled him a little and you could see it hurt him.

You would think it would be easy to stand over him and laugh, but I couldn't. You could see he was hurt, and I felt absolutely awful. I wasn't mad, and I couldn't enjoy seeing anyone hurt as a result of something I did intentionally. I actually watched a fellow player helping him off the field, and I told him I was sorry! He looked at me in a strange way, and I figured that now we would be in a big fist-fight soon. But it never happened. He stayed away from me and I stayed away from him from that point.

I wish I knew what became of him. I would like to think that he just grew up and became a man and changed for the better as I did. I'd like to think that he, like me, would do things differently if he could go back and relive his youth.

  I didn't know then what I know now... that if you can look into a man's heart and soul, and understand just who he is and how he got that way, you can't dislike him. Think about that. It is an unusual person who can understand that when they are 17 or 18. But if I could have just known what made him the way he was, if I could have just known how he got that way, chances are I could have scratched him off that revenge list I kept. Anyway, I am hoping for him nothing but the best in life, and hoping God didn't snuff him out, but gave him an understanding of what it means to love your enemies as he eventually did me. Oh to tell you the truth, I still get just as mad at times, and I rant and rave and get belligerent with someone I see as deserving of my wrath, and I forget 'Love Thine Enemies' until later and then I could kick myself. But the difference is, I know now that's what God asks of me, and I am to try my best to do it. I have made progress and I am proud of myself for doing it, even if I am a long way from getting there.

  In the two years I was at School of the Ozarks, I really saw lives change, and sometimes it was for the worse. There would be sessions in the lounge or in someone's dorm room when a dozen or more boys would get into big discussions about the Bible or Christianity. I realized right quick, after being in a session or two, how silly those debates were. I doubt if any minds were changed and looking back, some of it was downright comical. I didn't understand enough about the Bible or Christianity to open my mouth, but of course that never stopped me. I was always opening my mouth about something I never knew anything about. People wonder if God laughs, and I am telling you, if He was watching us as we had those heated debates about Him, He had to have laughed a little.

Nothing much changed me in college. I was clueless about most things, but to my credit, I clung to the things my dad taught me, and I adhered to the beliefs he had, and they became my beliefs too. He and the men he had for friends were a tremendous impact on me, as were the old-timers who came in the pool hall where I worked. At School of the Ozarks, I saw a devout young man who was the son of a minister, completely turn away from what he had been taught, and become as wild as any kid there, with alcohol behind most of it. I always figured that sometime in his future he would come back to the way he had been brought up, and I'll bet he did. But introduced to the short-term satisfaction he found in a way of living he had never seen, he liked it, and too many students probably thought it was a good indication that there was really nothing to Christianity.

But looking back on it, I believe strongly that my brain wasn't prepared at the age of 17 for understanding the complexities of Christianity, nor the simpleness of it. I don't believe God, the great Creator, looks at kids of that age and holds them responsible for much. He knew me better than I knew me, and I wasn't 'saved' at the age of 13 like that old uneducated preacher thought. I was in my mid-twenties before I really began to understand the teachings and the directions of Jesus. I made a conscious decision I wanted to follow Him as best as I could when I was in my late twenties, and it wasn't done on an emotional trip to a church alter, it was done slowly, over a period of time as I thought and talked to God when I was out in the woods or on the river alone.

I believe that kids who are like I was at the age of 17 or

18 are looked upon by God the Creator as his children. I was given special attention not by what I was or what I deserved, but because of prayers of devout people like my maternal grandmother and my folks. I was given time to know what is true and real in this world. I always asked the same things for my kids, and I have seen God answer prayers beyond the shadow of a doubt, time after time, for all who come to Him.

As a parent, you try your best to help your kids understand what you stand for, to understand your convictions and beliefs. You watch them go away to college or the armed service or into life in whatever way, and you pray. If you have that faith in God, you see results in the lives of your children. But you have to wait! And you have to be patient. Patience is something I have always had trouble with, even back then when I was the Prince of Point Lookout.

Chapter 8

IN TROUBLE EARLY

If I recall, I was working one morning at Dr. Clark's home late in the summer when his secretary, Jan Hoynacki, called to tell me I was wanted immediately in Dean Todd's office, and I needed to get there quickly. There was one reason people got called to the Dean's office, and that reason was... you were in trouble. You had done something wrong and it was something bad. You had better go there with a repentful attitude and your hat in your hand and a long sad face making it plain that whatever the heck you had done, you were sorry, or it was an accident, or you couldn't remember a thing about it. I liked Dean Todd... a lot. He was friendly and ordinary and talked about things on a level of the students. And he and I already had one experience I wanted to forget. It had happened only a short time before that late summer day, when my good friend Bob Carr and I were goofing around playing practical jokes on one another. For some reason I got the idea it would be really funny to put an egg in his pillow. It worked! About eleven o'clock that night, Bob lay back for a good night's sleep and that cold egg busted, making him think that his brains had drained out one of his ears.

Dean Todd helped a lot of students to stay in school and I was one of them. I could have been sent home several times if he hadn't been willing to bend a little and give me another chance.

Mrs. Swenty, of course, was called upon to replace the pillow that night, far after her bedtime, and as much as she liked me, she had little choice but to report the incident to the dean's office. And that is when I met Dean Todd. He smiled just a little when I came in and shook his hand, maybe because he could see my knees knocking together.

But he regained his Dean-like composure quickly, with that look of dismay and perturbition. I figured he was about to ask me if I had a way home. Instead he asked me if I liked S of O and I spent ten minutes telling him why I loved it so much.

Then he kind of looked off into the distance and asked me why, if I liked it so much, that I would do so much in such a short period of time to get myself expelled?

I threw myself on his mercy, and proclaimed that from that day forward he would see a changed man. I said I had seen the error of my ways and would never ever do anything out of line as long as I was there and maybe even longer. And then I really went too far, in exclaiming that if Bob Carr hadn't have put a blackberry bush under my sheet, I never would have done that thing with the egg. I could see why much of the blame should be placed on ol' Bob.

Dean Todd got up and lit his pipe and walked around behind his desk. "I'll bet that briar bush hurt didn't it?" He asked.

"Yes sir", I replied. " I think I have even got a briar or two stuck in places on my body right now that I can't get to."

"But the thing of it is, Bob didn't damage or destroy school property," Dean Todd said, "and you did, and that's why you are here. What you did ruined a pillow and a mattress."

"It is tough to get egg yolk out of a mattress," he pointed out.

I hung my head, and then came up with an idea. What if I was to buy the school a new pillow and a mattress? I pointed out that the army salvage store back in Houston had both, and on my next trip home I could get a couple of the better ones and bring them back!!

Dean Todd puffed on his pipe and nodded his head. He said he thought they could buy both there in Branson, and if I would agree to pay for both, he thought he could see a way to let me stay there and prove I wasn't no account and worthless by cleaning up my act.

Dean Todd and Dr. Clark, photographed while having a discussion in the Dean's office. They may have been discussing whether or not I should be kicked out of school for putting an egg in a fellow student's pillow!

the school with the agriculture boys a full day on Saturday.

The cost of the pillow and mattress was a problem, since I didn't have enough money to buy a pair of socks from that army salvage store, but Dean Todd worked it out to where I could haul hay in the field across the river from the school with the agriculture boys a full day on Saturday. I was in the clear after that, with the debt paid and all forgotten as long as I never ever saw the inside of Dean Todd's office again.

But there I was about two months later, heading for his office all over again. I just decided I would go in there and plead innocent to whatever it was I had been caught doing, and if they kicked me out of school I would take it like a man and jump off the bluff there overlooking Taneycomo.

Dean Todd could see I was expecting the worse, and he shook my hand and grinned at me and told me not to worry, I hadn't done anything wrong. He introduced me to two men in dark suits, and told me their names. He said they were insurance investigators, and they wanted to talk to me. Uh-oh!! I had gone from the kettle into the fire. I might have to get an education in prison!

Chapter 9

HAY-HAULERS

Back in my high school days, when I didn't have many friends, I met a young man in the pool hall by the name of Neldon Neal. I am using his real name because I have nothing but good things to say about him. When a person is my friend, he is always my friend.

Neldon had no father, and I don't know why. He had about six brothers, most younger than he. I only knew two of his younger brothers, and they seemed like great kids to me, but his older brothers were a rough bunch. When I was a senior in high school, Neldon's oldest brother, who was likely close to thirty, came out of the corner bank one Saturday morning, to see his estranged wife and her mother there before him. I don't know what the details of the argument were, but apparently he had been an abusive person, and he threatened his wife as they argued. Her mother stepped from the car with a pistol, and shot him several times. He died right there on Main Street.

Neldon's family was having a hard time of it, with their mother working at different jobs to try to get them all an education. She had to be a heck of a woman, though I never met her. Her sons all had names starting with "N". Neldon, Nelton, Nolan, etc. Neldon could have been a bully, with his background. He was tall, built like a rock, and he looked a little like Clint Eastwood looked when Clint was young. He was always polite, dressed well, and was respectful to older people. He really liked my dad and my family. Neldon and I met when I was about to become a senior in high school. He was a year older than I and out of school, working at one job and then another. He had no social life either, so the two of us ended up on the river quite often on Friday and Saturday nights, fishing. But on Saturdays that one summer we hauled hay together, bucking bales for about 3 or 4 cents a bale, if I remember right.

A local lady had a regular crew she depended on, and it wasn't long before Neldon and I were her top hands. I considered him one of my best friends, but I knew there was a dark side to Neldon. He spent most of his time with a big smile on his face, but it was deceiving. Neldon was tough, and when he got mad, he had a look to him that scared me. I understood him, and if it hadn't have been for my dad I might have been helping Neldon plot ways to get even with people back then. The two of us considered ourselves as outsiders, always poor, always looking at the local rich people as enemies. At one time I think we both had lists of people we were going to come back and get even with someday, and that is a fact.

One Friday during that summer Neldon spent the night with me, as we were going to go fishing at daylight. We went to town to get something about 8 p.m. and on the way home we came upon a truck involved in an accident which was full of watermelons, and many of the watermelons were in a ditch. We stopped to look, and a lady who said the watermelons were hers, was giving some to folks who were helping. Neldon and I picked up two or three and went home.

We had been asleep for an hour or so that night when someone started banging on my folks' front door. Dad got there first, and turned on the porch light, stepping out on the porch. There before us was a kid about my age who likely was the lowest most worthless piece of trash Houston ever produced. He thought of himself as a tough guy, but he was cowardly and sneaky in everything he did. There were two of his cohorts with him, and they started in about how they were going to kick me around that front yard if I didn't give them the watermelons I had taken.

Really, it was a scary situation, because I was barefoot, and there were three of them, and I didn't figure I could whip any two of the three. Truthfully, since I was only about 5 foot 7 and weighed about 150 pounds, I wasn't even sure I could whip one of the three. But I also was thinking, that with my Model 12 Winchester shotgun hanging on my bedroom wall it wasn't likely I'd be giving them a damn thing. It was a very dangerous situation. Dad always told me that someone scared really bad was more dangerous than someone who was mad.

Neldon, who had not yet came out the door, heard all of it before he got outside, and when he came out on the porch he didn't even stop. Barefooted and with fists clenched, he just walked out into the yard toward the car.

I heard my dad say, "This is something you boys can handle, I'm going back to bed." That was a good thing for those three hoodlums, because at the time he was about 6 foot 3 and 230 pounds, strong and lean and only 35 years old. They didn't want to make him mad. They weren't really after a fight, their idea was to go back to town and brag about how they came to our house and made me give them some watermelons in the middle of the night.

Neldon waited 'til he heard the door close, and you could see that the three idiots who expected only to find me there had no idea they were about to become involved in dealing with Neldon Neal. Each of them knew all about the older Neal brothers, who wouldn't look kindly on anyone threatening any of their younger siblings.

I saw a different young man that night in Neldon. He walked up to the tough kid who figured on terrorizing people, and he said several things I can't print here. Then he told them that he was going to let them run off as quick as possible and he was going to find his tennis shoes and put them on and we were going to come after them. He said that when he and I caught them they would be in the next week's newspaper as missing dumbasses, and no one would ever find any of them. He not only scared them, he scared me.

When we got our shoes and shirts on we got in my old car and drove back to town, and I prayed we wouldn't find those guys. Of course we didn't. And word got around that Neldon and I were good friends, so it made life easier for me. Not only did I have my cousins, the McNew brothers to back me up, I was a close friend of Neldon Neal.

I really liked Neldon and his younger brothers, and when I went away to college, I kept looking them up when I came home. That summer I was a freshman at S of O, I went home as often as I could when haying started, and Neldon and I made lots of money bucking bales. I was surprised when Mrs. Swenty summoned me down to take a call one night, and Neldon was on the other end. He was practically begging me to come home and help him put up several hundred bales that weekend. He said it would just be the two of us, and if we could do it, the guy would pay us a hundred dollars each.

Making a hundred dollars in one weekend was just unheard of when I was 17. I told Neldon to get things arranged, and if I could get the money in advance I would work beside him, daylight to dark. I knew a little about the guy we would be working for, and he had been in the used car business at one time. Handshakes with the guy were no good.

I hitchhiked home on Friday evening and got there before dark. Neldon had my money, and we went down to the river and built a fire and fished 'til midnight, then got up before daylight and headed for the hayfields out east of Houston. We had talked it over and figured we had to get a little more than half the bales in the barn that Saturday, so I would drive the old one-ton truck, easing it along in double low, granny gear. As I came to a bale I would jump out and throw it up on the bed without even stopping, while the old truck groaned slowly along, then jump back in the moving truck and guide it to the next bale.

It would have been a tough thitng to do with regular bales… but…these bales were wet. A week before we had a big rain, and they had been soaked. Of course, as most

everyone knows, wet bales don't dry out in the sun, they just mold inside and become so hot you can't hold your hand down inside the bale without burning it. And wet bales are so heavy you have to be a horse to handle them. From time to time, I would just get so worn out that we would switch jobs, but all day both days, that old truck was easing along, motor groaning and gears whining, as we loaded it again and again, and stacked the hot, wet, heavy bales in the old barn back in the middle of nowhere.

By the time we finished on Sunday afternoon, I'm guessing it was a hundred and fifty degrees in that barn. But I was so naïve I never thought anything about. I said 'so long' to Neldon, and with that hundred dollars in my pocket, set out on Highway 63 hitchhiking back to school. I never saw or heard from Neldon Neal again. I have no idea what happened to him, but those insurance investigators in Dean Todd's office made me realize that he was in trouble. And so was I if I didn't have the right answers.

They told me the barn had burned, and the owner was trying to collect a bunch of insurance money on it. They wanted to know what I knew about it, and I told them. The thing that saved me was that I had only received my hundred dollars for the work, and I had never met or talked to the owner of the hay, though I knew him. It became obvious that what I had to say, if I told the truth, would hurt Neldon. He may or may not have known what was going on, but it was a cinch that he had dealt with the owner of the barn, and knew what he was up to.

They told me they believed me, and had already checked my new, meager bank account back in Houston, the only one I had ever had. They said that if they needed me, they would be in touch. When I left, I asked Dean Todd if that was another mark against me. He grinned at me, and said that he was thinking about calling me in every week just to check up on me, and what I had been doing.

About forty years later I was watching the news one evening and I heard that authorities were looking for a man by the name of Neldon Neal who, in the heat of an argument, had shot and killed his wife. It was a stunning blow. They said he was hiding out on the river, and there was a massive manhunt underway. I thought to myself that it was me who showed him all the caves and taught him how to subsist on the Big Piney. It took weeks to find him, and finally his son talked him into giving up, or he might still be out there. Today he is serving a life sentence in the Missouri State Penitentiary, and I got a letter from him saying he was a different man today, because there, he had learned about the Bible, and someone who forgave men of their sins when no one else would.

While I was S of O, I never made another trip to the Dean's office. Dean Todd said from time to time when he would see me on campus, that he missed having me come by. I got to know him a little better as time went on and he was a good guy, a friend to the students and a credit to the college.

Chapter 10

DR. NIGHTINGALE

At the age of 17, a kid isn't capable of making mature decisions, and part of the problem with this world today is that society constantly wants to look at 18-year-old college kids as adults. Maybe some are, but not many. When you are 17, as I was when I first came to School of the Ozarks, you are more than likely easy to sway one way or another, especially if you haven't had strong role models and good parents in high school. And I am convinced that young adults who wind up addicted to drugs or alcohol, or involved in some kind of petty crime that leads to greater offenses, go one way or another because of the influences of good or bad people.

I have already written about Dr. Clark, and his influence on me, but I know beyond a doubt that I owe much of what I am today to a botany teacher at School of the Ozarks by the name of Dr. Alice Allen Nightingale. She was old and suffered from arthritis, which made it difficult to climb stairs and spend hours on her feet in a classroom. She wore flowers in her braided gray hair, almost always, something I suppose that came from the time she had spent studying and teaching botany in Hawaii. She didn't appear to have much sense of humor, and I didn't like her much at first because of that somber disposition, a complete lack of tolerance of any tomfoolery among students. I have already written about how Jay and I ended up on her bad list when we decided we would race from her class pretending we were firemen at the school when the campus siren went off. I knew good and well she didn't like me because... well, just because! I figured if I was a teacher, I wouldn't like me either.

One morning when class ended, Dr. Nightingale stopped me. She asked me if I had to be in class or at work and I said no. Then she sort of started complaining because I made so much noise walking on those hardwood floors with shoes that had steel taps on the soles. "Why do you put those things on your shoes?" she asked. "Don't you know what kind of noise they create when you walk?"

I was indignant. In America, a person ought to be able to wear anything he wants on his feet unless he is going to church, or walking on a basketball court! Besides, I hadn't put them on those shoes, they were on there when I got them at the School's clothing commissary, where you could buy clothes and shoes which had been given to the School for needy students, for only about fifty cents or a dollar. I had bought several shirts there and one good pair of denim jeans. I would have bought more, but that pair of jeans I bought gave me three pair. Who would need more than that? The shoes were shiny and black and only a little bit too big. I was wearing them in that photo of Jay Johnson and Darrell Hamby and me in front of Foster Hall, found somewhere in this book. In Branson, a pair of shoes that good would have cost ten dollars.

I think Dr. Nightingale had no idea. She sat there a moment and just looked at me, with a little bit of surprise

Dr. Alice Allen Nightingale, the S of O Botany instructor. A little gruff, a little cranky at times it seemed to me, but one of the greatest influences on me as a boy. She had a tremendous impact on my life and if she wasn't an angel, then I never knew one.

on her face. She told me she was sorry she had made such a big thing of it, but she said I should take them to Mr. Swenty and have him remove those steel pieces on the soles, or otherwise I would never be able to sneak up on anyone, or sneak out of class. That made me smile, and I'll be darned if she didn't smile too.

Then she told me that she lived in a little cedar glade to the south of the campus, and she loved to work on her flower gardens and shrubs and create new places for new plants. But she said she was getting too old to do much of the work, and she asked me if on occasion I would like to come and work for her. She said she would pay me a dollar and thirty-five cents an hour. Boy did I jump at that!

At Dr. Nightingale's home, I dug and I planted, and I moved some rocks out of her lawn and some other rocks into her lawn. I'd fix it the way she wanted, and then when she changed her mind, I would refix it the way she wanted. I would usually work after school, because I went back home every chance I got. But on those weekends when you were required to stay on campus, I might work a little on Saturdays and Sunday afternoons.

She was a grouchy old lady at times. She'd asked me for my opinion and then tell me why it wouldn't work and we would do it her way. Looking back on those times, I think Dr. Nightingale was in pain a lot, but she never said. We would have some great arguments at time. Usually she tried to teach me something every time I worked with her. In class we were studying plant taxonomy, and she was trying to teach me how to key plants with a step-by-step procedure in the book. I would have never developed the interest in plants in her classroom that I did around her little cedar glade home. I came right out and told her that I thought calling a red cedar tree a juniperus virginianus was ridiculous. "What would my dad think," I told her, "if I told him I wanted to go out and help him find a juniperus virginianus for a Christmas tree?"

She told me that there were no cedars in the United States, that they were junipers, and the only true cedar trees were found in foreign countries like Lebanon and Israel. She explained how many times common names were confusing, while the genus and species names given to plants and mammals and fish and all other living things identified them down to a very fine point. One instance she pointed out to me was how I called a squirrel scampering across her lawn a 'red squirrel'. What I didn't know was that there was an entirely different squirrel in the far north also known as a red squirrel. I began to understand. Then we would have some lemonade and cookies and she would explain what was behind the idea of scientific names, and how species were named for places they were found or how they looked or who discovered them and that kind of thing. It was something I had no interest in, and then suddenly I was captivated by it. How she did that with me is amazing.

One of her laboratory assistants was upper classman Mervin Wallace, who many years later reminded me what a dumb kid I was when I took my first class under Dr. Nightingale, and how perplexed she would get with me. Mervin, whom I am convinced tried to kill me by loaning me a capsize and chaos canoe he owned, said I once told her that if you had seen one plant you had seen them all. I don't remember that, but it was certainly something I might have said when I was 17.

Once she began to talk about plant evolution. Raised

in a little country church, that hit a nerve with me. Right there in class I spoke up and told her she could talk about evolution all she wanted to, but I believed in God and no one was going to convince me he didn't create the world and everything in it. Her answer was, "Mr. Dablemont, I will be seeing you after class, so don't you leave until we have a little talk."

I figured she was going to kick me out of class, but she didn't. As best as I can remember, she told me what an idiotic statement that was. "Do you think I have any less of a belief in God than you?" she asked. I told her it was pretty obvious she did if she thought that walnut trees might have evolved from buttonbushes, and chickens came from dinosaurs.

She told me to shut up and listen and I did. She talked about how evolution was nothing but a slow, slow change. She said she was convinced that God had never stopped creating, but continued to help all things he had created become stronger, better able to survive. "I believe in a God so great He still creates, every single day, and he sees the change He makes in the creatures and plants on the earth and says, 'it is good'".

I don't say I accepted all she taught me readily, but no one had ever made me think like Dr. Nightingale. And no one ever made me want to learn like she did.

Two years out of college I was working as Chief Naturalist for the Arkansas State Park system trying to create a naturalist program at four big parks, which included the state park on the Buffalo River. I took three of the young men I had hired as park naturalists, to spend an afternoon talking with Dr. Nightingale about keying Ozark plants and plant taxonomy. She asked me what I thought she could do with them in only a few hours that would make their visit worthwhile. I told her that it wasn't so much that I wanted her to teach them something, but that I wanted them to meet her, possibly to be inspired to learn and know more, as she had inspired me. Her face beamed when I told her that. In all the time I knew her, I never really thanked her and I regret that. But one of these days when I find the great, beautiful garden in heaven that Dr. Nightingale is in charge of, I intend to give her a big hug, and do just that. She was not only a great lady, but a great teacher, and I am convinced God planted her right square in my path to help make me a little better person.

Her good friend on campus was Dr. Poole, and I suppose they were both approaching 80 years of age when I was there. She introduced me to him and told me he needed someone to do work on his place from time to time. I told him that I was the right kid for the job, as Dr. Nightingale had trained me well and he couldn't get many students to work as hard as I would for a dollar and thirty-five cents an hour, paid at the end of each work session. I think Dr. Nightingale may have told him I could use the money, as I needed a new pair of shoes!

Dr. Poole was a foreign language instructor and he spoke with a precise manner that seemed strange to me. He had white hair and a white mustache, and looked a little like I thought Mark Twain must have looked. He never took a full-length step, he just shuffled along. He lived on campus in a little house in a row of homes along the east side of the entrance road, and behind his home was a thicket growing along a tiny little creek which fed the lake they called Lake Honor. I don't suppose anyone had ever fished in that small concrete lake with a big fountain in the middle of it, but I asked Dean Todd if it would be okay if I did, and he shook his head as if he couldn't believe someone wanted to fish there, and said he didn't know of a single rule against it. I'll tell you the difference between Dean Fry and Dean Todd. If I had asked Dean Fry, he would have found some rule to prevent fishing there. I am not saying he was a bad sort, but he seemed to look at his job as a position to subdue students who were like me, making us conform to what a student at S of O ought to be. I never understood him, so of course I never liked him much. But who wouldn't like Dean Todd? The man was just a common sense kind of guy, who knew where lines should be held and where rules and regulations ought to end. If Dean Todd kicked someone out of school, he deserved it. He bent over backwards to be tolerant and flexible.

Well, there were bass in Lake Honor. I learned that if I were to keep the secret to myself I should fish there a little after dark and I never kept any fish. They were plentiful, but not big, maybe up to two pounds, but they really fought hard. But I digress, ('digress' being a word I learned in a journalism class at S of O). Working on that little trickle of a creek for Dr. Poole, I helped create, over a year or so, a beautiful little garden covering a half-acre or so behind his home. With him doing the planning, and me doing the work, we converted thickets into places for exotic plants, made a little dam to form Dr. Poole's pool, and set sculptures here and there. By the time I left, it was a beautiful little place, the spot where I took my future wife on our first date, something I was very proud of. Of course it was school property, and when Dr. Poole died, some nitwit had much of it destroyed. If they would have turned it over to the school gardener and landscaper and his crew, it could have been something to last for decades, for campus visitors to see and enjoy as a tribute to Dr. Poole. But as the years went on, different leadership came to the school, and progress took on a different look. All I can say is, you should have seen it. In the various seasons of the year, it was always a peaceful, beautiful place. And often, a man can take real pride in the making of things which do not last, but have their place in a period of time that makes youth have a simple and true value.

If only I could have hunted ducks on Lake Honor. Imagine my surprise when I found out it was full of bass even though none exceeded 15 inches. Looking back through library files, I was surprised to find out that I had written some outdoor columns for the School newspaper, and one of them was urging students to turn back bass they caught from Lake Honor so they could grow. I'll bet there were some lunkers there in time, after I was no longer a student. I am tempted to sneak in late some night and try it again now.

Chapter II

NETTIE MARIE'S BASS

My roommate, J.B. King was a good guy, and we got along well, but it wasn't long until he became close friends with some of the student firemen he worked with, and moved to the other dorm. Ms. Swenty asked me to move from my room in with a fellow I had seen a time or two around campus with a guitar, singing. His name was Ronald Jay Johnson, but he preferred to be called by his middle name, Jay.

Truthfully, I thought he was about half goofy. You never knew what he was going to come up with. I didn't know it at the time, but he was one of the most creative, talented young men I ever met. Girls on campus loved him, because he had thick curly black hair, was good looking, and seemed to ooze self-confidence. He also seemed never to express a serious thought. We had that one thing in common, we both absolutely loved to laugh, and we were constantly dreaming up something to bring some humor to life on the campus. The photo shows the two of us doing a comedy skit, which we wrote and put together some time during the second year I was at S of O. We were the very first performance on the stage of the newly opened Nettie Marie Jones Learning Center, and maybe the

Jay and I clowning around on the stage of the auditorium at the Nettie Marie Jones Learning Center in the summer of '66, I think.

worst one ever. Jay was playing the part of long-time St. Louis Cardinal announcer Harry Caray, and I was a lame-brained, not-so-important bench player on the team. I can only remember one line of the skit, in which he asked me if I had any children. My answer was, "Sure 'nuff Harry, I have three beautiful children…" and then continued, "and two ugly ones."

At the time we did that, I was scared to death. It was the formal celebration of the opening of the learning center and the students were putting on a sort of 'evening of talent', where for a couple of hours there was music, drama and comedy. The place was absolutely packed, and my heart was beating a hundred miles an hour. I noticed the little sheet of paper Jay held with his questions on it was shaking like a leaf, but we got through it somehow, and we got a few laughs. While we had the distinction of being the very first act ever on the stage of that auditorium, I imagine no one remembers that but Jay and me.

Before I go on with all the good times and adventures the two of us shared, it might be a good time to brag about my contribution to that big beautiful learning center, which held the auditorium and two or three floors of classrooms. Nettie Marie Jones was a very rich lady, probably in her seventies, and she had given a great deal of money to the school. I am sure she didn't pay for the entire huge building, but there's no telling how many millions she gave.

While it was under construction, it was a great place to sneak off with a girl and explore the dark stairways at night, and I think I did that a few times but not often enough. I can't remember the names of the girls. If I did I wouldn't tell. Now some girl from that time can read this book, and brag to her family that she was one of them! Whomsoever

The newly finished Nettie Marie Jones Learning Center, 1966.

they were, I just know we were scared to death of getting caught.

At seventeen, I was very naïve and immature. This isn't one of those tell-all books, and if it was, I wouldn't have much to tell. It was very exciting to just take fifteen minutes to kiss and hug some girl and get away with it. The only exploring I ever did, had nothing to do with the girls I met and spent time with. I was happy to just hold them close and smell them, and steal a few kisses whilst exploring the vast stairways and darkened rooms and get away with it. You have to remember I never did anything like that in high school, having never had enough money to have a date. At S of O, you didn't have to have much money to explore the under-construction learning center, or sit on lookout point watching the moonlight on Taneycomo, far far below.

And yes, I certainly did have a big part in the financing of the big learning center that bore her name, because I took Nettie Marie Jones fishing!

I didn't know who she was at the time. Dr. Clark quite often benefited from the trout I caught from Taneycomo, and he told me about property on Table Rock Lake only about four or five miles south of the school called "Clevenger Cove". There was an old V-bottom aluminum boat there, a great deal harder to paddle than our johnboats on the Big Piney. Still, I could paddle it, and that cove back then was full of big bass. I'd spend a weekend there on occasion and bring bass filets back for Dr. Clark, telling him I would take him fishing whenever he would like.

He never seemed to have any time, and then all at once he did. He told me that he needed me to paddle a boat around Clevenger Cove one spring evening for him and a guest of the school, to see if I could help the elderly lady catch a fish.

On the Piney, I had been guiding fishermen since I was 12 or 13. Guiding fishermen was my cup of tea. So there I was about 4 p.m. one beautiful afternoon in April paddling around Clevenger Cove with Dr. Clark, the only time I ever saw him without a suit and tie, with a lady along whom he referred to as Mrs. Jones. I didn't know who she was and I didn't care. My job was to see to it she caught a bass, because she never had caught anything before. Dr. Clark's tackle was sparse, and he only brought some little Zebco push-button reels on rods that would have been better suited for goggle-eye fishing than bass.

Mrs. Jones couldn't cast, no matter how hard I tried to teach her. My favorite topwater lures were going to be of no value. Thankfully she was just enjoying the afternoon so much she didn't seem to care about the fishing. So I tied on a plastic worm rig for her, a hairy jig for Dr. Clark, and took them out just off the timber aways so they wouldn't get hung up. I paddled slowly along while Dr. Clark's line trailed out on one side and Mrs. Jones' line trailed out on the other side, behind the boat.

I was paddling and daydreaming, maybe about spending some more time that evening in the vast dark stairways of that new building with a new girl I had met. I couldn't figure out what the heck the two fishermen were discussing, it had to do with finance and interest, and investment and that sort of stuff.

All in all, it was a really boring afternoon, until Dr. Clark interrupted himself and jerked his rod high. It bent double and he fought a two-pound largemouth around, whooping and hollering and laughing in that Georgia accent, until he got it close enough that I could grab its lower lip and boat it.

The two of them acted like that bass was a wall-hanger, and I put it over the side of the boat on a stringer, thanking God that something exciting had happened that didn't involve any one falling out of the boat and getting wet.

We had a fish! There weren't going to be any more, I knew that. I had that plastic worm rigged so that the hook's barb was back deep in the plastic. It would keep Mrs. Jones from hooking every stick on the bottom of the lake she dragged over, but if a bass picked it up, she'd have to set the hook, and she had as much chance of feeling a strike and setting the hook in a bass as I had of making an A in algebra.

Everyone is a witness to a miracle on occasion. Some of us recognize one when we see it, and others do not. For instance if some tourist were to come along and fall off the rocky lookout point at the school and bounce off the ledges and limbs below, finally coming to rest at the edge of Taneycomo Lake 200 feet below, and then climb back up complaining of little more than scratched knees, that would be widely recognized as a miracle by about everyone.

But if some little old lady in a flowery dress holding her purse in one hand and a ten-dollar Zebco rod and reel in the other hand were to hook and land a big bass, I'd probably be the only one in the country to know that God or some of his angels had a direct hand in it. But shucks, wasn't Peter a fisherman?

Take my word for it, it was a miracle! I was watching her line, and I saw the fish hit. There wasn't any doubt about it, the line didn't just stop a bit, it lurched. And then it cut through the water to the left a bit, and came back.

"Ma'am, jerk that rod a bit," I hollered. She turned to look at me, and the end of it started to bend. "Hang on to it ma'am" I hollered again, "and give it a jerk."

Mrs. Jones never once jerked, but thank goodness she did hang on. The line was good and strong, the knot was good, and the fish had somehow or another wanted to eat that plastic worm so bad he set that strong hook deep into his jaw.

Mrs. Jones didn't look all that hefty. I figured a three-pound bass would whip her. But she came alive in that boat, struggling and squealing, turning that handle on the reel backwards, giving that bass a little more line to work with. I finally got it across to her to reel it the other direction, and there was pandemonium on Clevenger Cove.

It took awhile, and there was great suspense as all three of us thought there wasn't a way in the world she would

That's Nettie Marie Jones in the center, receiving an honorary degree with Dr. Clark on her left and Reverend Schimpf on her right. This is several years after I took her fishing and she caught the big bass.

get that bass close to the boat. But by golly she did, and I being the type of experienced professional fishing guide I was, got ahold of his lip on the first try. He weighed five pounds if he weighed an ounce and there has never been three happier people in one boat.

That afternoon back at Dr. Clark's house, there were pictures taken and all the girls who worked there looked at me as if I was a hero. But after I filleted the bass, I headed back to the dormitory and a supper of meatloaf at the cafeteria, remembering the laughter and happiness behind me at the Clark home. Kind of sad, ain't it.

A few weeks after that trip, the head of the landscaping department, Dave Barker, brought me a fertilizer spreader, a little device on two wheels like a lawn-mower without a motor, and he left several sacks of fertilizer, and the instructions of how to fertilize Dr. Clark's lawn by filling it and pushing it back and forth covering the entire lawn equally. Dave didn't stress 'equally' quite enough. I kept forgetting where I had been and where I hadn't, and the result was a lawn that had some green stripes and some yellow stripes and some brown stripes. The green stripes meant I had applied just the right amount there, and the yellow stripes meant there had been a little too much applied, and the brown stripes meant there been way too much applied.

Dr. Clark had to explain to every guest he had coming that the kid he had working for him was better at fishing than farming. Dave Barker saved me by coming over and resodding the whole thing, recreating a beautiful lawn.

In the wake of that, there was a good chance I would have been transferred to the boiler plant or the cannery had I not had one strong supporter.

Mrs. Jones had donated a hefty sum of money to finish the learning center, in the name of that young man who took her fishing. Dr. Clark told me that she had gone on and on about what a polite and thoughtful young man I was, and how hard I had worked to make her happy on that fishing trip, and how I was an outstanding example of what School of the Ozarks was all about. I don't know if it ever got put down on paper, that big contribution given in my name, but I can tell you this, it sure saved my butt when I made Dr. Clark's lawn look like the bottom half of the United States Flag.

Unfortunately for all of us guys who had no place to take a girlfriend while the construction was going on, the Nettie

Marie Jones Learning Center was quickly finished early that summer, the lights went on inside, and they locked up the doors at 8 o'clock each evening.

It has been years since I have seen it, but thousands of students have gone through the classrooms of that big building, and graduates who learned much there, have gone on to do great things. There is a big bronze plaque on the outside wall with Mrs. Jones' picture engraved on it, and information about her, and the generosity of her giving. But nowhere is there a plaque stating my contribution to the Nettie Marie Jones Learning Center, nor has anyone ever given the proper credit to that big bass that gave himself up for the advancement of education. No one but me!

Chapter 12

JAY JOHNSON

Jay Johnson was tremendously talented. He had a quick wit, and a great sense of humor, and a real gift when it came to music. He kept me entertained in the dorm singing and playing the guitar, and we were always trying to come up with the lyrics to a song that would make people laugh. About that time the college was looking for a school song, and they decided it would best be done through competition. Jay wrote a song which he entered in the contest and if you ever go to a basketball game or some event at today's College of the Ozarks, you may hear it. His song won and Dr. Clark awarded him the first prize check when it was first played in 1966.

Unbelievably, several years out of college, Jay wrote a number one song, sung by several famous singers, but made a hit by Dickie Lee, a pop music singer of the 1970's. It was number one on the national charts for weeks, and if you listened to the radio at all, you have heard it. He called it "Rocky".

Remember the lyrics? "Rocky I never had a baby before, don't know if I can do it... but if you'll let me lean on you, take my hand, I might get through it." It was a real tearjerker, but I think Jay laughed all the way to the bank.

The song was number one on the pop music charts for quite awhile and it won Jay a gold record. He donated it to the School of the Ozarks museum, and he laughs about the fact that the first time he came back to see how it was displayed, he had to pay to get in.

In time, Jay got into radio as a big-time D.J. that almost everyone in the Ozarks has listened to at one time or another.

He has worked for years under the name of Woody P. Snow, finally retiring just before this book was published in 2015, in order to do some writing and artwork. Today we still get together on occasion, and our friendship is strong. He has published one novel, entitled "Blood Silver" and is about to publish another, entitled, "Depraved". Amazingly, he paints Ozark scenes and has sold several of his paintings.

But at School of the Ozarks you would have never known of his brilliance. He helped me plan some of the goofiest things two students ever got into. The hamster fiasco in the following chapter was just one of many. We had a class together under an elderly teacher by the name of Dr. Alice Allen Nightingale, who taught botany. They said she had taught college plant taxonomy for years and lived for a while in Hawaii. She came to S of O after retirement age, and she was a great lady and a great teacher. The first week in her class I had little regard for her. A year or so after I got there, I loved her. I will say more about her later, but that lady was an angel, and I never meant a person ever who knew more about botany. Few people have had more impact on me than Dr. Nightingale.

Jay and I sat next to each other in her class, and it was he who came up with the brilliant idea of getting out of class when the fire alarm sounded. The student firemen on campus would bolt from class like a thief leaving a liquor store, with books and papers left behind tearing up big chunks of green lawn on a mad dash to the fire station. Jay thought we ought to do the same thing just for kicks, the next time the siren wailed. I was all for it, wished I had thought of it myself.

We had only been in botany class for five or ten minutes that morning that the fire alarm sounded. I think I jumped over two desks and Jay knocked over the waste can as we imitated student firemen intent on getting to the fire in time to save some widow and her pet cat. In the dorm, we relaxed and laughed and laughed. We had fooled Dr. Nightingale and every student in that class.

The next class session, two days later, Dr. Nightingale gave her lecture as always, and gave no indication she even remembered what we had done. Shucks, Jay and I were convinced we could get away with it every time. As the bell signaled the end of the class, I was arranging my books and notes when I heard her say, "Oh by the way, Mr. Johnson and Mr. Dablemont, will you stop by my desk for just a moment as you leave."

Puzzled, we obeyed, and Dr. Nightingale seemed busy organizing her desk for the next class, not even looking up at the two of us as she said in her quiet, slow voice, "I am very much aware of the necessity of our campus fire department, and I have a list here of those students who make up that group. Surprisingly, I have found neither of you are on that list. So should you ever again bolt from my class with the sound of that awful siren, please just keep on running and do not bother to return to this class."

She stopped then and looked directly at me, and asked, "Do we have an understanding about that, Mr. Dablemont?"

I could only stand there and nod my head with my mouth open, feeling a little like I did when I got caught drawing a naked woman on the blackboard in the grade school library years before. Jay and I grew up a little that week. We started to get the idea that this wasn't grade school.

One of the dumbest things the two of us did was learning to stage a fight just like they did on some television western. We practiced it, and got it down to a fine art. There was a French boy who lived on our dorm floor, and we decided that we would try our act on him.

Oh it worked all right. Why did I have to be the one who was winning the fake fight? The young man with such a beautiful French accent and pleasant gentle personality, decided that Jay needed help, and he planted a good right hook on my left jaw. I saw stars for a while, and it took lots of convincing from Jay to keep him from following up on his anti-bullying effort.

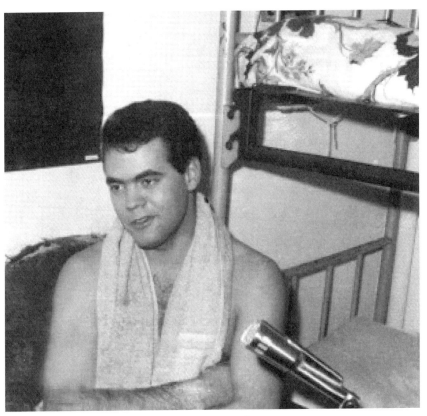

Jay Johnson in our dorm room. Somewhere in that wall is the hole our neighbors used to fill the room with cigar smoke.

Chapter 13

THE RAFFLE

Ms. Swenty put Jay and me in Room 222, which looked straight out over the campus from the exact middle of the dorm. You could look straight south right up the big sidewalk that led to the chapel. It was a great view, and our room was next to the stairway that went down to the lower level and was right across from the shower and toilet.

Having access to that water came in handy when we decided to remove the window screen and throw water on students collecting on the porch below, which we did on occasion. If you did things right, they never knew what room it came from.

Jay and I hit it off, even though he didn't know a thing about the outdoors and I didn't know a thing about music. And music was all he wanted to talk about. He could write songs, sing like Ricky Nelson, play the guitar, and tell you all about musical people from Burt Bacharach and Johnny Mathis to John Lennon and that weirdo in England, Elton John.

From the time we moved our stuff into Room 222 we were having fun. I don't doubt that if we had not been roommates we would have improved our grade average by a half point. But life would have been boring. It was while

I was rooming with Jay that I got in trouble for putting the egg in Bob Carr's pillow.

In no time at all, Jay formed a band with guitarist Dane Allen, from Thayer, Missouri, and Billy Wagner, a drummer from Detroit, Michigan. Billy Wagner looked like one of those guys on the movie John Travolta made when he was young, "Grease". Billy had that same kind of hair, and Jay said it was the way to look if you wanted to have girls interested in you. It wasn't long until Jay and I were singing Everly Brothers' songs and I had changed my hairstyle at his instruction.

Larry Dablemont   *Jay Johnson*

But even with a new hairstyle, I wasn't of much interest to girls on the campus at S of O. But I didn't need to be. Back in Houston, Missouri, my sister Muriel, who was fourteen, had a friend by the name of Linda the same age who all of a sudden didn't seem like such a little girl. She was my first girlfriend and as a college freshman, I took her on the very first date I ever had. We had been going to church at the Houston Free Will Baptist Church since I was about eleven. I think when I got kicked out of the fifth grade, Dad started worrying about me becoming a juvenile delinquent and we found that little country church. I always suspected that Dad thought the Free Will name on the church meant if you were too poor to donate any money into the collection plate you didn't have to, but really, Dad wasn't that much of a skinflint. It's just that, like me, he just never did accumulate much money he didn't have a use for. Anyway, Linda's folks went to that same church and knew me fairly well, so every time I took Linda somewhere on a date, her brother and my sister went along. And since I only got home about every three weeks it was a doomed romance. I wrote her lots of love-letters but her mother always edited them before Linda go to see them. That first romance didn't last long, as Linda dumped me for a local guy who had a new car, and soon I had another date with a girl from S of O. Before long I just went wild, sometimes having two or three dates a month.

My dad always insisted that I go to Sunday School and pay attention to the Ten Commandments because I needed to know what was right in my life. He insisted that I remember three things he expected of me. "Don't lie, don't cheat and don't steal," he would tell me often. There were other things less important. I remember him telling me that if he caught me drinking or smoking he would break my neck. He said those things would kill me, at which point I stressed that a broken neck would likely kill me too.

But the thing about lying and cheating and stealing was something he stressed often. Then one Saturday we floated the Big Piney hunting ducks, and Dad had bought a contraption called a Silver-Trol electric motor to put on the boat, hooked up to a big auto battery. When the wind came up and paddling was hard, or when we had our limit of ducks, he would attach the little motor to the back of the wooden johnboat and we'd clip along about as fast as a man could walk. What an invention!

That first day we had it, Dad stopped on a gravel bar for lunch and while we ate he told me that mom thought he had borrowed it from one of the old guys at the pool hall. But in truth he had bought it for twenty dollars, which was a heck of a deal.

We both knew that mom had to skimp on perfume and dresses and shoes, so if she found out we had put out that much money on that little motor, she would hit the ceiling. Dad said that I should never reveal we had paid for it. If mom asked, it was borrowed.

I thought about that for a moment, and then I told him that that would be a lie, and he had always told me not to lie. Dad sat there on a log in his patched hip boots, smoking his pipe and gazing toward a distant river bluff. Finally he spoke. He said he knew that the bible said to always tell the truth but he said there was a very important section where Jesus was giving a direct sermon and he said, "Blessed are the peacemakers." Dad allowed as how, if mom found out what he had done, there would be no peace around our house at all. It was better, he said, to tell a small lie when it was necessary to be a peacemaker.

Jay had the same kind of family, the same kind of values that I did. He came from Wentzville, Missouri, and he talked about his folks with respect and admiration. But at S of O, we were a long way from home.

It isn't like the great hamster caper amounted to lying or cheating or stealing. It was a little bit of all three, but not a whole lot of any of them. I don't know where he got it, but shortly after we became roommates, Jay snuck in a beautiful little golden colored hamster in a cage. She was tame and gentle, and would let you hold her and pet her and she didn't bite a whole lot, and never very hard. She was a great little pet, very easy to take care of, very quiet, and very pregnant.

We didn't know that until one morning a few days after Jay got her, we woke up to find about eight babies in her cage, in a nest of chewed up paper and fur. It was a predicament. Jay got a hold of a little book on hamsters that told us we needed to separate them from their mother at a certain age, and put them in a cage and feed them to a stage of their development when we could surely sell them for two dollars apiece. If Jay kept 60 percent, as owner, and I got 40 percent, as the assistant owner, we would come out with an amount somewhat better than either of us had in our pocket at the time. The whole thing of course, had to be done without Ms. Swenty's knowledge, as it was illegal to have a pet.

Right off, we knew we had to deal with the two guys in the room next to us, Mervin Wallace and Cecil Hampton. They were the kind of guys you may remember from your college days. Both were athletes, long distance runners on the S of O track team. Everyone thought the world of them, and truthfully, I tried awfully hard not to like them and couldn't. Over the years I was proud to call them friends.

But as a distance runner, Mervin was tall and thin, and if you would have put a black mustache on him he would have looked like Snidely Whiplash. Cecil was quiet, and well spoken and polite, and his girlfriend was Julia Clark, the beautiful girl who drove the black thunderbird, and was Dr. Clark's youngest daughter. I might have had a chance to take her to the movies if it hadn't been for Cecil… a good reason to dislike him strongly.

With the coming of the hamsters, both Mervin and Cecil, who were Ms. Swenty's favorites in the whole dad-blamed dormitory, had something to use against us. They had no reason to want to get revenge except for the fact that someone had thrown water on them while they were on the porch. It could have been someone from any of a half-dozen rooms, but they chose to think Jay and I had done it, without a shred of solid evidence. A tension had developed, and the revenge factor loomed large.

We made a deal, agreeing to be at the behest of the two of them in some future endeavor, which might involve our aid and assistance in a non-financial way. In return, they would remain mum on the subject of illegal baby hamsters.

Jay and I were free to develop a plan, which would finance a new cage for the quickly growing hamster brood. We had to raise about $7.50 to purchase a cage of the required dimensions in Branson, and the idea we came up with was brilliant. We went to the girls' dorm, and sat out on their porch and showed pictures of the babies to a few of the girls, telling them what a bad situation we had on our hands with no funds for a new cage.

Of course, they wanted to help by chipping in some small change, but Jay wouldn't hear of it. "Ol' Larry and I are too proud to do something like that," he said, "Unless there was some way to pay you back."

That was my cue, and I had rehearsed my part. "Maybe we could have some kind of raffle," I said, "and draw names and fix it so the winning girl could have a date with Zeke Morbel or Alphonse Garosh." Those of course are not the real names of the two guys who were looked upon as 'ladies men'. I hesitate to use real names here, knowing people have been sued for less.

Both those guys were good-looking upper classmen, and both had girlfriends.

Jay pointed that out. It would never work, he said, but then, snapping his fingers, he came up with another idea.

"You and I don't have girlfriends, and you aren't likely to have any any time soon," he said, "we could take the winning girls to the movie in Branson on the school bus, and throw in all the soda pop and popcorn they could put away, on us."

I can't believe it worked, but somehow it did. In every group of young girls, even really smart ones, there are enough gullible girls to sell a couple of dozen raffle tickets with the prize being a date with the two of us.

At this point, you would think everything was peaches and cream. But what a mess it became, more like persimmons and vinegar. First of all, the mother hamster, that sweet, gentle little pet... ate every darned one of her babies in a couple of days. It was a hard thing to accept. There would be no hamster auction, no windfall of profit from the sale of the babies.

And then as it turned out, the girl who Jay most wanted to take out bought four tickets and put them in the name of the ugliest girl in the dorm. The one I wanted to take out wouldn't even buy a ticket! So there we were a week later with fourteen dollars we would have to return, unless we could figure out how we could rig the drawing so that we could take the two girls to the movies who seemed to be the best applicants according to looks.

The announcement was to be made on the front porch of the girls' dorm on that previously designated evening. We

Jay was big into music and theatre, and performed at the School Theatre which was under the direction of Dr. Clark's son-in-law, Joe Embser. The productions there attracted attention from all over the Ozarks. He became a radio personality in later years by the name of Woody P. Snow.

didn't do a drawing. We just told the few girls assembled there that we had let Mervin Wallace pick out the names from a coffee can. He was respected and trusted, and even the most skeptical of the rafflers wouldn't say much if we got it over quickly and got the heck out of there.

It hurt some to realize that most all the girls who had put money into that raffle did it mostly to get a cage for the baby hamsters, rather than to win a date with Jay and me.

The one girl on campus that I idolized was Pat Decker, the prettiest, quietest, nicest, little redhead I had ever seen. Several times I had tried to talk to her, but just couldn't get my nerve up to do it. Naturally, with her name on a ticket, she is the one who won the date with me. One of her friends had to come down and tell me that Pat couldn't go to the next Monday night movie on the bus with me because she had to study for a final exam.

I sent her back up to ask Pat if she would be able to go the following Monday night movie, and she sent her friend back to tell me she couldn't go that night either, because she needed to study for a final exam again then.

Well, even at that age, I didn't have to be beat over the head with dead hound to be convinced the foxhunt was over.

Jay didn't get to take his pick to the movie either, as she quit school and got married the weekend before the next Monday night movie.

We got to keep the fourteen dollars. I got half because we couldn't figure out how to divide fourteen dollars in a 60-40 split. I think somebody snitched on us, as Mrs. Swenty demanded we get rid of the hamster. I probably ought to point out that Mrs. Swenty was a wonderful lady, and too soft to be a dorm mother for boys our age.

I came down the stairway with the hamster cage that Sunday morning, and she was waiting, with her arms crossed, a stern look on that pretty face, a patsy if there ever was one.

"You found a place for it, I see," she said firmly.

"No ma'am," I told her, "I'm going to let it loose behind Dr. Clark's house on the bluff. They like that kind of habitat. Jay is afraid she won't make it once it gets cold, but I imagine a hawk will get her long before then. I'd druther a hawk eats her than a doggone blacksnake. I hate snakes... still, she'll have a few days of happy life, even if she does miss this little wheel she likes to run on."

Word spread around campus that I was a heck of a salesman, to get five dollars for that hamster cage from Mrs. Swenty. And I know she really enjoyed that little hamster. Jay and I got to visit it from time to time.

That's me on the left, wearing those shoes Dr. Nightingale didn't much care for. Darrell Hamby is in the center and Jay Johnson, AKA 'Woody P. Snow' on the right. After fifty years, I still keep up with both of them, and we remain close friends.

At Dr. Clark's home, I was the afternoon shift, mowing the lawn, taking care of grandkids, cleaning out the gutters and swimming pool, and driving Dr. Clark to the airport and back. I also ran errands for the girls who worked in his kitchen, tested the cookies and baked goods they made, and occasionally provided trout and squirrels for Dr. Clark and his wife Elizabeth.

Standing on the point overlooking the Taneycomo Lake Valley to the north at the west end of the campus in 1965, all dressed up for something. I almost never wore that clip-on tie, but I had it for years just in case I needed it. Compare the valley beyond me to the photo to the right, taken in 2015 and you can see what development has taken place in the past 50 years. I liked it the way it was when I first saw it.

Three special people here... Julia Clark to the left and Jay Johnson to the right. They are going over a play to be performed at the school summer theatre. The fellow in the center is Fred Pfister, who was a couple of years older than me. His folks' farm was just a few miles from me when I was a boy, and his brother Jerry was one of my closest friends. Fred married a girl he met at S of O, went on to receive a doctorate degree and return to teach at School the Ozarks for several years. Until his retirement he was the editor of the Ozarks Mountaineer magazine. He is a fine writer who today writes a regular column for the Journal of the Ozarks, and still lives with his wife Faye only a few miles from Point Lookout.

There weren't many photos taken of me at S of O, but that first summer I was there I spent one weekend at the swimming pool working as a lifeguard. No one drowned! A photographer took this photo of me in 1966 and it was used in the Schools' publication, **The Ozark Visitor** *in that summer. The pool was enclosed after I left, but I will never forget having to take a swimming course there in September and October in which we all darn near froze to death because the water was so cold.*

Librarian Mary Anna Fain was a character. She didn't like me at all. Once I wore a red and black shirt into the Library and she nearly came apart. She told me to go change that shirt immediately because red and black were the colors of the devil. In my years in high school and college, I got kicked out of three different libraries! Today my books, all nine of them, are in each. If Miss Fain knew I had my books in her library she would roll over in her grave!

Terry Williams worked at the guest house next to Dr. Clarks home and gave me cookies she made on occasion. I would have married her too, but she had a boyfriend by the name of Eric Spyres who became a good friend of mine. They were big into the theatre and music part of S of O, and they both taught music and speech and acting after graduation as a married couple. Their children, a daughter and two sons, became well-known actors and opera singers, traveling around the world, performing in opera houses all over, even performing in Carnegie Hall. I think Carnegie Hall is in New York!!!

Dr. Clark gave me this autographed picture of him when I left S of O, and I treasure it still today. I think I knew him very well, and if you added up his pluses over his minuses he stood out strong and tall. I am proud to say he was my friend.

George Richardson, a friend from back on the Big Piney River, came to S of O one summer before I left and talked me into getting into a canoe race on Taneycomo, out of Branson. We won, and I still have that little trophy. The 40 dollar prize we split didn't last long.

My sister Muriel was the valedictorian of her graduating class in high school in 1968 and graduated as the valedictorian of her class from S of O in 1972. She later received a Master's Degree, and became a licensed professional counselor eventually retiring as a counselor for the Blue Springs School District. At School of the Ozarks she met her husband, Jerry Wood, who grew up in Cushman, Arkansas. She and Jerry, who is a Viet Nam war veteran, have three boys and live happily today in Lee's Summit Mo., where they are retired to play with grandkids.

Muriel was remembered a little better than I was, proof that athletic ability and academic ability is most often passed on to the second child in a family rather than the first. Returning to School of the Ozarks homecoming celebration one year in the early '80s, people would look at my name tag and ask... "Are you any relation to Muriel?". She is shown here receiving an academic award from Dr. Clark. She worked for Dr. and Elizabeth Clark in their kitchen during her four years at S of O.

My younger sister was quite an athlete. She is shown here with some of her teammates on the School of the Ozarks girls track team

Chapter 14

JULIA, CECIL AND MERVIN

The beautiful girl with the long, black shiny hair that I had met that first weekend at the entrance gate driving the Thunderbird, turned out to be Dr. Clark's youngest daughter, Julia. It embarrassed the heck out of me when I met her on my first day of work and she remembered me, the guy at the entrance gate who was trying to impress her, and did way too much talking. Julia was an S of O high school senior. She was quiet and unassuming, but the envy of the whole campus because of that 1957 black Thunderbird. When I got to know her, I really liked her. She had lots of record albums, and she gave me a couple that she knew I liked, one of them an album by Johnny Burnett, that Jay and I enjoyed listening to on his record player.

Anyone who got to know Julia well did indeed like her, especially Cecil Hampton, who was a college freshman living in the room next to Jay and me. Cecil was Julia's boyfriend, and I don't know how, if opposites attract, that the two of them ever got together, as Cecil was as reserved and quiet as she was. But years afterward, the two of them were married, and I hope someday they both read this and are living happily ever after.

Julia Clark *Cecil Hampton* *Mervin Wallace*

Cecil's roommate was Mervin Wallace, who had to be one of the most liked and respected upper classmen on campus. He was Dr. Nightingale's lab assistant, and was a botany major who made the most of his education. Only recently, I learned that Mervin today owns and operates a big garden center nursery, the Missouri Wildflower Nursery at Jefferson City, Mo. with his son. Like Cecil, Mervin never said much. He was all seriousness and had the discipline of a monk. Both Cecil and Mervin were stars on campus not just because both were A-students, but also because they were genuine 'track stars'. They competed everywhere against many other colleges, and usually won. Cecil ran shorter distances, like the half-mile, and Mervin ran the one-mile and two-mile events.

Mervin had a hard time understanding people like Jay and me, because he was so serious and dedicated and we were anything but that. But he did have a good sense of humor in that he had a wicked grin every time he looked at one of us. Most of the rest of the time Cecil and Mervin were too serious and Jay and I tried to cheer them up a lot, like the time we dumped water on them from our dorm room over the porch. I think it was meant as a feeble attempt at light-heartedness when they started the "We Hate Jay Johnson Club", a loosely organized organization which quickly gathered quite a few members. They had a once-a-month meeting where they sat around and tried to figure out ways to get him kicked out of school or sent to jail, or worse. It didn't worry Jay much.

As serious as we thought they were, that rascal Mervin drilled a hole between their room and ours with a star drill, and stuck a little tube in it. It came out behind a dresser, so Jay and I never knew a thing about it. He and Cecil would sit in their room late at night and smoke a cigar and blow the smoke into our room through that hole. We never ever knew where all that smoke was coming from. We just sat there and coughed. Mervin loaned me his canoe a time or two, just for the asking, though once his canoe nearly killed me. I will talk about that adventure in the next chapter.

Cecil and Mervin were, as I said, well-respected scholars and athletes, and not just runners, but stars. I myself was something of a runner. In fact I was pretty doggone fast. When I was a freshman at Houston High School, Coach Weaver had us timed in the 100-yard dash and I was the fastest of all of them. But because of my jobs after school, including the one in my dad's pool hall to make ends meet for our family, I never did get to go out for any sports. At 5' 7", and 145 pounds, I wouldn't have been much good at football and basketball, but brother could I ever run. I mean, for a few seconds, I was FAST.

My best time was in a big field down close to the Piney River, when I ran the hundred-yard dash in about 9.4 and a big black bull with horns behind me ran it in 9.8! I told Mervin that, and he at least grinned a little. I told him that when he went out some evening to run that long course he ran every single day, I wanted to go along. With another one of those evil grins, he said he would be glad to have me join him. So one spring night about an hour before dark, when he started his two-mile run, I pulled on my sneakers and a pair of gym shorts and followed along. Mervin Wallace wasn't very big around anywhere. He was better than six feet tall, and my thighs were bigger around than his waist. Oh yes, he was endowed to be a runner and me trying to run with him at first look, might have appeared to be a ridiculous endeavor. But I knew I could do it.

Mervin's course headed north from our dorm, down past Dr. Clark's home downhill to Taneycomo, not far from where we fished for trout. I jogged along beside him, joking about how easy it was and speculating that I might join the track team myself. Then we got to a big level field that bordered Taneycomo Lake and reached almost to Highway 65. I will admit it was a little harder to run on that rougher ground, but Mervin, not saying a single word, had to be awfully impressed that I was right there with him, taking two strides with my short legs compared to one stride he took with those long thin 'nothing-but muscle-and-ligament' legs. I wasn't having a bit of trouble keeping up on that downhill course. Then we got to a long flat field and it got a little harder. At the end of that long field, a small road headed back toward campus, up a grade that passed the School of the Ozarks' dairy farm.

That's about when I looked up and couldn't find Mervin. He had ran off and left me. I hollered for him to wait up, just long enough for me to catch my second wind, but he was way out of hearing distance, and then he was gone, like smoke off a dying campfire. And there I was, all alone and exhausted, unable to jog another yard. Walking was becoming painful, up that hill. I wasn't sure exactly how to get back to the dorm and it was getting dark. It was not, of course, getting dark on Mervin, who was already back at the dorm taking a shower.

I thought to myself that surely Mervin would send help back to find me, to get me and my tired aching legs and my throbbing lungs back to civilization. Surely he wouldn't leave me there. I staggered up into familiar surroundings some time later, and figured out that the dorm was less than a quarter mile away. Gathering every ounce of strength I had, I put one leg before the other, with burning cramping muscles pushed to their limit. Gasping for breath, I crumpled onto my bunk at my dorm room. Jay was playing his guitar singing, "I'm five hundred miles away from home".

Mervin Wallace was one of the greatest distance runners S of O ever had on its track team.

I had a little problem with leg cramps that night, and the next morning Mervin wanted to know what had happened to me. I told him that I had gotten disoriented and ran all the way to Branson, then up around Hollister almost to the state line and back to the dorm, a distance of about twice his run. I told him I had arrived about 30 minutes after he did. Mervin grinned as he always did, and asked me if I would like for him to talk to the track coach about getting me on the track team.

"No," I told him emphatically, "not just 'no' but 'heck no'". I told him I just didn't have the time, with the studying I wanted to do to improve my grades!

While Cecil and Mervin were as different as day and night from Jay and me, they were great neighbors and we only became better friends as the semesters rolled by.

Julia's older sister, Liz, was married to the head of the theatre department at School of the Ozarks. His name was Joe Embser, a very witty intellectual type, but a very large man. Liz was very thin and they made an unusual couple. They had two sons, Ricky who was about six and just as intellectual as his father, and Darwin, who was about four, and probably smarter than me, but not as smart as his brother. However, he could swim like a fish. I hadn't ever seen a little kid who could swim like that, and it was my job on occasion to drop everything and watch the two boys when they wanted to go swimming. Those two little boys were a part of my job that I enjoyed most. Dr. Clark had a swimming pool and patio just to the north of his home. The pool wasn't real big, had a low diving board on one end. When the boys wanted to swim, I used the little dressing room next to it to put on my swimsuit and watch them. I was a certified life-guard, and worked as such on occasion in the summer at the big S of O outdoor pool to gain extra hours.

One summer day I was sitting on the Clark's diving board watching the boys swim, marveling at how both of them could swim so well, especially Darwin. That little shaver could swim the length of the pool without taking his face out of the water, and he loved to show off how good he was at it. I was his best audience.

That afternoon he started across the pool and just went to the bottom, feet first, still trying to swim. For a moment I thought he was clowning around and I said to myself, "I wonder how he learned to do that?" Then I realized he was having trouble getting to the surface, and I went in after him. When I came up, he was clinging to my neck like a lizard to a fence post, sputtering and gasping. The little guy just all of a sudden wore himself out I guess. I mentioned it to his mother, but I don't think she ever knew the seriousness of it. No one ever knew it but Darwin and Ricky and I, but I saved his life that summer afternoon.

My job, when those two little boys needed me, was a great job. They were both cute as the ears on a bug and hilariously funny. One afternoon when Liz had something to do with Mrs. Clark, I took Ricky down into the field below the school, next to Taneycomo Lake. Mr. Miller, the head of the S of O Museum, said that field was known to be the site of a large encampment of early men, way back a few hundred years. The field had been plowed and rained on, so the conditions were perfect for finding arrowheads. I had found a few there, nothing spectacular, but always fascinating to me. We found a few more that day, and I let Ricky find the ones I spotted, maybe two or three partly broken points, but he was excited about them. Of course

Darwin found all kinds of little rocks that were nothing but chert flakes or chips, and I acted like they were really something.

Then all of a sudden Ricky picked up an oblong smooth rock that had actually had a thumbhole ground out of it. It was a grindstone, perfect in all ways, worn on the bottom from years of grinding whatever the Indians were grinding in that campsite. You might know he was enamored with it. I offered him a really nice arrowhead I had in my room, and he wouldn't take it. Then I got his attention with a whole dollar bill. Ricky was wavering. I threw in a Snickers candy bar. I almost had a trade, but he said his mom wouldn't let him eat candy bars! The answer was simple. I would hide out three Snickers candy bars out in the patio by the pool, and the three of us would eat them when his mom wasn't looking.

That grindstone sits in my office today, and every time I look at it I feel guilty. But back then, a dollar bill and three candy bars was quite a bit to trade, for a smooth rock. I wonder sometimes where those two boys are. They must be in their forties now, and maybe Ricky has a few of those crude, broken-tipped arrowheads we found. I haven't heard from them since I left college, and I don't know whatever happened to Cecil and Julia. I know they were married after he graduated and had kids of their own.

As for Mervin Wallace, I am going to go to that big well known nursery of his, up there in Columbia, and take him a copy of this book and see if he will trade me a few wildflower seeds for it. I may challenge him to a very short race!

This is why Mervin ran every evening... he seldom lost a race. I suppose I came as close as anyone, just wasn't familiar with the course!

Chapter 15

THE DUCK HUNT

That big stretch of water they called Taneycomo was fairly wild looking in the S of O area back then. Today it is over-developed and crowded with boats, but it wasn't in 1965 and '66. It had bunches of wild ducks on it in the winter. And remember that back home Dad and I were avid duck hunters. We would float the Big Piney River in a wooden johnboat with a blind on the front and slip up on flocks

I loved hunting ducks so much because back home on the Piney it was something we had always done, and when I saw how many ducks there were on Taneycomo, my enthusiasm for hunting nearly got me killed.

of mallards and woodducks with a quiet paddle and jump-shoot them.

I couldn't see why the same thing wouldn't work on Taneycomo. Dave Barker had a short V-bottom aluminum boat that I was sure I could paddle, and so he and I went out one Sunday morning at daylight and made a bow blind out of the cane that grew along the river in huge thickets. If I remember right, I paddled him down the river a couple of miles and he killed a few ducks, even though the boat was difficult to paddle.

Barker of course was the head of the nursery and landscaping department. He had a crew of young men working for him and he would come by from time to time and tell me things I should do on Dr. Clark's lawn. He was young, with a beautiful wife and a little two-year-old girl who could talk your leg off. Seemed to me like he had it made. He had a dry sense of humor and laughed a lot, just the kind of person I had always liked in the pool hall back home. I got to know him fairly well, and I took him and his best friend, Alex Warner, who was the science and biology instructor at the school, back home to float the Big Piney and camp overnight a couple of times.

Dave Barker's crew was a fun-loving lot. He had a couple of natural comedians working for him. One was a blonde curly headed wisp of a kid by the name of Gary Miller, who never said anything that wasn't funny. He claimed his mother was a lineman for the Green Bay Packers and he was born on the Chicago Bears' football field as a result of a blocked punt. I don't know what happened to him, but I always thought he might show up sometime on The Tonight Show. Of course, I provided the whole crew a big laugh when I tried to use the fertilizer spreader on the Clark's lawn and forgot where I had been as I spread it. The result was a lawn that had yellow stripes from too much fertilizer, and green stripes from where I had done it right.

In a couple of weeks after a good rain it all returned to green, and though Dr. Clark never said a word about it, I know he had to think I was the dumbest kid that ever came to S of O. Barker was asked by a school visitor what in the world had happened there, and he broke up his crew by answering, "Student labor!"

Visitors to School of the Ozarks often were amazed about the beauty of the campus. Dave Barker was the reason for that. He was a great work supervisor for a crew of hard-working students. I got to know him well because he loved to hunt and fished. He went back home with me once and floated the Big Piney and we hunted ducks on Taneycomo a time or two.

We went duck hunting on Taneycomo in December, that first year I was there. What I remember most is that Dave picked me up at about five in the morning at the dorm, and it was a cold clear night. I looked up to the heavens and saw absolutely hundreds of meteors falling through the skies from one horizon to another. In my 17 years, I had never seen such a thing and it was hard to stop looking. In that hour before the dawn, there were thousands of meteors falling, streaking across the sky everywhere, a beautiful and unforgettable sight.

Since Dave Barker and I had a little bit of success, I was anxious to try it again, and the answer was Mervin Wallace's canoe, which he had chained up there on Taneycomo below the school. That gravel bar was student-made. The college had a huge gravel-removing crane of some sort sitting there and they took gravel out of Taneycomo, something that would be illegal today I suppose. They had created a gravel jetty that went out into the stream about 40 feet, and then jutted upriver about 100 yards or so. It was a wide, solid gravel road actually, and that's where we all fished for trout. It couldn't have been more perfect for the students who wanted to fish. Mervin had got permission to leave his canoe on the water between the bank and the gravel jetty, chained to a tree. He said that if I wanted to use it, I could. So I talked Bob Carr into going duck hunting with me one December morning just before our Christmas break. As hard to believe as it might sound, I kept a couple of shotguns in my dormitory room all the time. I worked on old guns a lot for the museum, where Steve Miller was the curator. I will talk about Mr. Miller more, but he had found out I liked to work on guns and so he let me take one or two back to my room, and when I had free time, I would take them to Dr. Clark's workshop out beside his pool and work on them, mostly fixing or remaking stocks.

I kept my old pump gun in my room and an old single shot shotgun that I had bought from one of the other students for five dollars, so Bob and I had the firepower to hunt ducks, and Mervin's canoe gave us the ability to sneak up on them. But that canoe was tragedy waiting to happen. Today you couldn't get me in a canoe like that in mid-winter with the promise of enough gold to sink it. It was narrow and it was short, maybe 15-feet long.

I look back on that day and wonder how I could have been that stupid. I think Mervin figured maybe he could get Jay and me both in it at once and therefore have a chance at getting new roommates in the room next to him and Cecil after we had drowned. That was about the time that the "WE HATE JAY JOHNSON CLUB" was going strong.

Jay had better things to do on Sunday morning than Bob Carr and I did. I think he was singing in the chapel choir. But Bob and I went down to the bottoms and cut some cane to make a bow blind with, and set out to hunt ducks.

We darn near swamped that little tipsy canoe when we stepped into it, but somehow we got seated, with our shotguns beside us, and started paddling upstream to find some ducks. We were about 200 yards up Taneycomo when I saw mallards on the other side. Thank God they weren't out in the middle of that cold deep lake. I eased us over to the far bank and we opened up as they flew. I think we got one greenhead and I picked it up, careful not to lean any, noticing that sometimes the water came only a couple of inches from the gunwale.

That old single-shot gun Bob was using didn't eject shells very well, and Bob had a spent shot-shell jammed in the barrel he couldn't get out. He asked if I had a knife, so I eased my old pocketknife out of my pocket and tossed it toward the bow. It landed right under Bob's seat. He leaned around and to the right to reach down and get it, and we both lost our balance in that rickety little canoe as he did so.

Twenty feet from the bank, we turned it over!

There are a lot of things I don't remember well from those two years I spent at School of the Ozarks. Hitting that icy water on that cold December day is not one of them. It is a hard thing to describe, going from dry and warm to trying to keep my head above water, and gasping to catch my breath. If you want to get an idea what it was like, just go down to the creek and jump in with all your clothes on, the next time it is in the mid-twenties outside.

For just a moment, it hit me that my old pump shotgun was gone, and then it struck me that it is hard to swim in hip boots. We hadn't had the foresight to put in life jackets or even floating cushions, so there wasn't a thing to grab onto. But the bank was only about twenty or twenty-five feet away, and I made for it. Bob and I were a pair of physical specimens when we were 17 or 18 years old and

both of us were good swimmers. But you are less good of a swimmer in heavy coats and hip boots. I do remember that my quilted cap with earmuffs was floating nearby and I grabbed it and put it on, thinking it might make me warmer. It didn't.

The canoe lay on top of the water though submerged. I don't know why I didn't think to grab it and hold on to it and therefore eliminate the risk of drowning. I just knew that the quicker I got to the bank, the happier I was going to be, so I thrashed around the end of it and Bob followed. Nearly to the bank, one of my grandpa's sassafras paddles that I had brought to school with me, was right before me. I grabbed it and about the same time I did I felt the bottom with my feet. Looking back I saw Bob behind me, really struggling. It looked as if he wasn't making any progress at all, and going under as he fought to stay afloat. Without thinking, I just stuck the paddle toward him and he grabbed it and I pulled him to the bank.

We climbed up above the tree-lined bank, and there was a big grassy field before us. We stood there a moment, trying to get some air in our lungs, coughing up cold lake water as our clothing began to freeze and get stiff. I could tell by looking that we were both alive, and that surprised me, after thinking a few seconds earlier that I was a dead duck, just like that greenhead we had worked so hard to get.

Above us, maybe a quarter of a mile away, there was a small resort known as the Fall Creek Resort. For a mile or so upstream and downstream, there was nothing else but fields and woods. Today along the shores of Taneycomo, you can hardly find enough open ground to bury a dead cat, with all the development. But in 1965, the fact that we were right in front of a resort was something of a miracle.

Had we been a couple of miles from anything, I think we would have died that morning.

There was nothing to do but head for that little resort, and there was no discussion between us. I think we did stop for just a minute to pour the water out of our hip boots, and then began marching across that field, walking as best we could in frozen clothing that felt like a garb of cold cardboard. I didn't know it at the time, but if those folks who owned the resort had been gone that Sunday morning we would have both been dead as well. Dead because of something I never knew a thing about... hypothermia.

I guess it took about 20 minutes to get there and when we arrived at the front door, my mind was wandering. I was actually starting to feel warmer, and there was something of a calmness replacing the absolute panic and fear I had felt 20 minutes before. Bob and I just stood there, and then it came to me that I should knock on the door. I can remember the gentleman coming to the door, and the look of shock on his face. I can't remember much else. He and his wife got us undressed and wrapped up in blankets and brought us something to drink, but I don't know what it was. I am not sure it wasn't the very first time I ever tasted whiskey!

Those people saved our lives and I never ever saw them again I don't suppose. They fed us and kept us there for an hour or more, and the lady dried our clothes. I ended up with a bad headache and my body hurt like the dickens for two or three days, like someone had really given me a good drubbing. The gentleman there at the resort took us down to a boat dock in Branson and the dock operator loaned us a boat and motor to go back up and get Mervin's canoe. I thanked him, and told them both I wished I could pay them something but I had no money to amount to anything. It was something how those two men wanted to help and didn't care if I could pay them. Today along Taneycomo if you went to a boat dock and asked to borrow and boat and motor for free, you'd really get laughed at. But the Branson that today thinks of little else but money and lots of it, was a different place back then. The people there at the resorts and docks were people who grew up in the Ozarks too, instead of the entrepreneurs to come from northern cities years later in search of a golden goose.

I talked to the two of them, and thanked them as best I could, offering to take them duck hunting sometime! They both had a good laugh about that. Then I lamented losing those two shotguns, and the dock owner went back in a little side shop and came back with something that looked much like an anvil on a long rope. He said it was a powerful magnet they had used on occasion to get outboard motors off the bottom of the lake, and it would surely retrieve my shotgun.

Bob and I used the boat and motor to retrieve Mervin's canoe and take it back where we had found it. We got my grandpa's boat paddle and one of my gloves. I never did find the other one. But we hadn't dropped that magnet down two or three times until I felt it clank against something metal and we hauled up that single-shot Iver Johnson shotgun. We whooped and hollered about that success, seeing a gun I thought would be on the bottom of Taneycomo forever. And it seemed certain we would find the other one quickly. No such luck! For a solid hour we dropped that magnet in search of my old Winchester pump gun, and brought up nothing. It was getting late in the day and Bob was ready to give up. I let him out to walk back up the bluff to school.

He took our only duck back to the dorm and I returned to the spot where my shotgun lay in fifteen feet of water.

There are those who have said over the years I lack focus and quit most everything too easily, especially when it comes to work. Even today, when mowing the weeds around my place or tilling the garden, I usually quit before it gets done, and figure it will wait 'til another day. But not back then, with that shotgun involved. It was worth about 50 dollars back then, and today it is worth a good 500.

I should have marked the spot better. My heart was sinking as I resolved that I would never find it. I could have cried until I felt that magnet clink against something. And there it was. The only thing I can think to compare it to is when your football team is down by three points and you've got the ball on your own three-yard line with ten seconds left to go. You know how gosh-awful that feels, and how wonderful you feel when the quarterback throw a wounded duck pass up in the air and somebody on your team grabs it and runs it all the way back for a winning touchdown with time expired. That's a little bit how I felt, sitting out there in the boat as the sun set, holding that shotgun to my chest, thanking God for letting me find it, first of all, and secondly, for letting me and Bob not drown.

I ran the boat back down the lake to Branson, thanked the man profusely and hitchhiked back to school with that shotgun under my arm. Can you imagine a kid getting a ride today with a shotgun in his hand? I got back with plenty of time left to oil the guns and clean that duck. The next day I picked it and singed it and took it to Dave Barker and told him I wasn't ever going duck hunting again unless they had a summer season in some distant future.

Bob and I stayed close friends all the while we were at

S of O, but I noticed that on occasion when I got really enthused about something and he saw me coming he would head across campus like he was really busy, or duck into his dorm room and lock the door.

This is the view fifty years ago from the Lookout Point back to the south. Compare it to the photo to the right which shows Taneycomo Lake today. Typical of those who develop our lakes and waterways, there is no stopping until there is no room left to use. But you can see why we could duck hunt here in the mid-sixties... there were no people around at all in the winter..

Chapter 16

TRANSPORTATION

It wasn't hard to get a ride home from School of the Ozarks because so many people traveling through southern Missouri knew all about the caliber of the kids going to school there. If you made a big sign to put on your suitcase saying, "School of the Ozarks student to Houston, Missouri" then you wouldn't have to wait long for a ride. One Friday evening that first summer I had my work hours in, and had to go home to buck bales on a hay crew I often worked on. You could make about fifteen to twenty dollars a day in a hayfield if it was a good crew, and that was really good money. Of course, if I had clients wanting to float-fish the Piney, I put that first, but when it got hot and the river was low, bucking bales was the way to make money.

So one summer evening I stood out on the highway in front of the School and right quick a fellow pulled over to give me a ride. He said he was going through Forsyth and heading to his home in Bradleyville.

About that time, they were finishing the big highway that went from Branson to Springfield, which was one heck of a project. By my second year at S of O it was open, but that first year, you went to my little hometown of Houston on a winding narrow highway from Branson to Ava, then north to Mansfield. The fellow from Bradleyville was a nice guy and we had a good conversation until we got there. He took me a mile or so out of town, and let me out on the east side of a bridge where there wasn't a thing but the small creek and fields. I stood there for at least 30 minutes and there were only three or four cars that came past, none of them wanting to pick up a hitchhiker. Despite the sign on my suitcase, you have to recognize that I looked a great deal like a criminal, with these close-together little beady eyes of mine set way back in my face. Had I decided to be a criminal, and they would have made a movie about me like they did for Bonnie and Clyde, they would have had to look a long time to find an actor who looked as much like a criminal as I did.

 Back to the southwest, a huge storm was brewing, the lightning and thunder warning me that I only had a short time to get a ride or take shelter under the bridge. You talk about close, there was a strong wind hit me as I headed for the bridge, and big drops of rain splattering against the hot pavement with a hissing sound as a bolt of lightning crashed down a mile or so to the south. And that's when the miracle happened. A little bug of a car, some foreign made older model, came chugging across that bridge and stopped to pick me up. I got in and thanked him profusely. I said I didn't care where he was going as long as he would let me out where there was some cover.

 That little old foreign car outran the storm, and the driver said he was going to Houston for the weekend and would deliver me to my door, a home owned by his second cousin. I couldn't believe it. His name was Gilbert Elmore, known best to those who knew him as "Gib". I knew he was a distant relative of ours, but I had never met him.

Gib Elmore worked at the Shepherd of the Hills Theatre, which was set in a rural area out to the west of Branson, where he was one of the Baldknobbers in the nightly play they had all summer long. He didn't have many weekends off, but he was headed home for a special family event of some sort and intended to head back to Shepherd of the Hills on Saturday night.

He told me that I should get a car and just leave it off campus, as many other students were doing. Of course S of O had strict rules against students having cars, because if a kid could afford his own car, he could afford to go somewhere else to school. But I believe if you didn't bring your car on campus except to load it and go home to work on some weekends, you would be sort of overlooked by Mr. Swenty, who was the campus security man, in charge of keeping the student car traffic to a minimum. If you got caught with a car on campus however, the rules were clear, you were suppose to be dismissed and sent packing.

Gib told me that if I ever got a car I could leave it at the Shepherd of the Hills and he would keep an eye on it for me. He said he knew that some of the students who had cars paid for their gas by charging a couple of dollars to take other students home on weekends and bring them back to school. When he let me off at my folks' home that Friday night, the storm had nearly caught us. I knew that it meant there most likely wouldn't be any work in the hayfields the next day.

I talked to my dad about the idea of getting a car, and he said that my Grandpa Dablemont had a car that ran pretty good and looked really good on one side. It was an eleven-year-old 1954 Chevrolet, and Grandpa had sold it to the local junkyard because the other side back quarter panel had been crunched in by a guy who ran a stop sign. But the damage was all cosmetic, as nothing else was defective.

On Sunday, I talked to the junkyard owner, Roy Fisher, who went to our local Free Will Baptist Church. He said the old car was worth seventy or eighty dollars for parts, but since he had given only fifty dollars to Grandpa for it, he would sell it to me for that.

I had about thirty dollars at the time, and I told him I would find another twenty dollars somewhere and come back the next weekend. But that Sunday afternoon my dad took me out to the south end of town and let me out and went home. I know that sounds awful today, that my dad wouldn't give me a ride back to school, but you have to remember it was a four-hour round trip, and Dad never had enough money for that. He was just a shoe factory worker at the time, and gas was 27 cents a gallon.

With my sign on the suitcase, I got a ride pretty quick. The driver was drinking, and he offered me a swig, which I should have taken. It would have helped my nerves. I found out his wife had just run off and left him and he was really despondent. He was driving about seventy or eighty miles per hour and I was praying at that kind of speed myself, that somewhere a highway patrolman might be on duty along the highway. Where are they when you need them?

The guy kept the bottle under his seat and brought it out every few minutes when he would start to cry and cuss at the same time. He even talked about suicide. At Mountain Grove, I talked him into letting me out and he didn't seem to want to. He needed someone to talk to, he said. Finally he let me out near Mansfield, Missouri and I had to sit on my suitcase for a while beside the road. My legs were too weak to stand.

It was two weeks later that my Grandpa McNew loaned me the final twenty dollars to buy the car. I hitchhiked home and picked it up at the junkyard. Roy Fisher filled the gas tank, just to help me out, and I don't know if any kid ever was any prouder of a car. If you didn't look at that back quarter panel on the driver's side, it was a real beauty!

Gib Elmore, true to his word, found me a parking place where it sat all week long until weekends, and I would hitchhike from the school to pick it up. And when I went home, other students would pay me three dollars to take them to wherever they lived, Mountain Grove or Ava or Mansfield or Cabool, and take them back on Sunday evening. Once I had eight of us in that old Chevy. In a short time I had made the fifty dollars that it had cost me, and I paid my grandfather back the money I owed him.

When Jay Johnson and I became roommates, he talked me into taking him to the Springfield airport to meet one of his girlfriends who had flown in to spend a week with some girls at School of the Ozarks. It began to snow that night and in little time it turned into a blizzard. With the nearly bald tires on that old Chevy, I don't know how we made it up and down those hills on the new highway from Branson to Springfield. Looking back on it, I think it was a miracle we made it.

I remember once when Jay and I went to my home for a weekend and floated the river and spent a night camped on a gravel bar. When we returned my car to its place at Shepherd of the Hills it was a little after midnight and we walked down the highway toward Branson for nearly an hour and didn't see a single car. I know that if you look at that busy and bustling metropolis today you can hardly believe that could happen, but it is the truth. Branson in

1965 was a town that hadn't yet figured out the riches that tourists could bring.

Taneycomo wasn't much developed back then, but there were little cottages being built on its banks at Branson. One of them was a place owned by our dorm mother's husband who was both postmaster at the School's post office and nighttime security officer. Mr. Swenty hired three of us students to dig his entire septic system right there only a few feet from Taneycomo's flowing waters. It was easy to do because it was mostly sand. We put in a septic tank and septic lines heading toward the lake, in only a few hours. In the 1970's with Turkey Creek carrying raw sewage out of Hollister, Taneycomo became a very polluted body of water. I wonder if the Swenty's septic system, which we put in, is still being used today?

Chapter 17

DARRELL HAMBY

When Jay Johnson decided to leave School of the Ozarks and pursue his music career elsewhere, it was a sad time for me. I couldn't imagine having more fun than we had as roommates. Jay had taught me very little except how to comb my hair different. He convinced me that as homely as I was, I had some attributes that could be attractive to a girl, even if those girls weren't as good looking as the ones he ran around with. He had become an extremely good friend, and I figured I would never see him again. That wasn't the case of course, as we have gotten together often in the past couple of years to see who can come up with the wittiest quips and create laughs just like those good old days. For awhile, I did a radio program on the outdoors for the same station where he worked as one of the most popular radio personalities in the Ozarks, known by his pseudonym, Woody P. Snow.

It was a sad day when he left, at the end of my first year at the college. The "I Hate Jay Johnson Club" that Mervin Wallace and Cecil Hampton had founded suddenly was defunct, and there I was alone in a dorm room next to those two, knowing I wasn't going to win any practical joke contest outnumbered that badly. As completely different as

Jay and I were, my next roommate was about as much like me as anyone could get. His name was Darrell Hamby, and as much as he had a reason to be sad and withdrawn, Darrell wasn't that kind of person. He had lost his brother a few years before at School of the Ozarks, when a hay truck backed over him at the school's barn. I think he may have been the only student ever killed at the school. I could see how close Darrell had been to that brother, and another one who was in the military in Alabama, and his dad. The only one of his family still at home was his mother, who was aging and in poor health.

On a weekend visit to his home, Darrell's fiancé snapped this picture of us with my old car's good side. It was the driver side that was all banged up.

He also had a girlfriend back home he was about to marry, and he and his girlfriend got me in a fix once. Darrell and I went back to his home at Piedmont, Mo., quite often where he had some great fishing. I had never met a kid so at home in the woods or on the river. And he had a lot to show me. We fished a place called Carter Lakes, and the Little Black River. We kept planning to go to Clear Water and Wappapello Lakes, not far away, but we never did. Of all things, Darrell Hamby had spent much of his boyhood and he could shoot snooker and pool both.

There was this one time I will never forget, when we took a weekend trip back to Piedmont in my old '54 Chevy, hauling five other kids and dropping them off in their hometowns for the standard three dollars each. That's when I first met his girlfriend and her family, a whole bunch of backwoods folks, who were like the people I knew back home on the Big Piney around Houston. His girlfriend, Sharon, fixed me up a blind date with one of her friends, a senior in high school, and the two of us went out on Saturday night with her and Darrell.

Truthfully, I didn't expect much. A girl who would go out on a blind date because she didn't already have a date on Saturday night had to be fat or ugly or both. But what the heck, while I wasn't fat, I had a pretty good idea I was just a notch or two away from ugly myself. So on Saturday afternoon Sharon and Darrell took me over to meet her, a redhead with blue-green eyes by the name of Sharon Slater, and she was absolutely beautiful. My knees got weak and I swallowed something. I think it was my Juicy Fruit gum, but I said hello even though I was about half-choked. If there is such a thing as love at first sight, I was afflicted with it. Later in the evening Darrell and I got all dressed up and I splashed on about half a bottle of British Sterling and combed my hair with a big splotch of Brylcreem.

This is a good place to say that back then the Brylcreem hair stuff had an advertisement on television... remember it? It was a little jingle put to music that went... "Brylcreem, a little dab'll do ya." Well because of that ad, folks have always pronounced my name the same way, Dabblemont. The name is French, once spelled Dableaumonte, and meaning 'dweller of the mountains' in France, where my ancestors came from the French Alps. But the name is pronounced like cable, table, fable, etc. It is Dablemont with a long A. And if I could meet the guy who came up with that little jingle I would likely punch him in the nose unless he was bigger than me.

At any rate, we showed up at Sharon Slater's home and her dad came out on the porch to meet me. He said it was hard to trust any boy that was a friend of Darrell Hamby, but he laughed when he said it. To tell the truth I think from what I saw over the years that folks in that little east Ozark mountain town of Piedmont all loved him.

So I shook his hand, noticing it was about twice the size of mine, and he was a foot taller than me. When he said he wanted his daughter home at midnight, I took him seriously. We had one great time that night... went out to eat at the local hamburger joint and then rode around the rest of the evening with Darrell driving, and Sharon and I in the backseat. It didn't take long to get over being afraid of her. She was a sweetheart, one of those girls who made you think you had known her for years. I couldn't get over how good she smelled, and how pretty she was. If this was what blind dates were supposed to be, every guy ought to have one.

But then came the scary part. About ten o'clock we went to a Sam A. Baker State Park, a beautiful place where the moonlight shined off the water, and whippoorwills called from the nearby woods. I have never known two hours to go so fast, as we listened to music, went for a walk along the lake and talked and talked. And then we got back into the back seat and I may have proposed marriage for all I know. I can't remember much about it until I heard Darrell say that we had a flat on one of my back bald tires.

We opened the trunk, knowing we had a short time to get the flat fixed and get Sharon back home. And that is when it came to me I might be about to die at the hands of her father... THE SPARE TIRE WAS FLATTER THAN THE ONE ON THE CAR!!!

There was only one thing to do. Darrell and his girlfriend set out to walk about three miles to the home of some folks he knew to try to get an air tank, or at the very least, borrow a car to get Ms. Slater home, where I was about to be shot.

Hamby's popularity there really came in handy that night. But truthfully, I wish he had been gone 'til daylight so I could have spent more time with Sharon. I figured it this way... if her father meant to kill me, he might as well do it the next morning as in the middle of the night. There were no cell phones back then, but Darrell's wife to be, used the phone at the home they walked to, and called Sharon's folks to tell them what had happened. Thankfully the spare tire held air, and I changed it all by myself because Hamby was so mad at having to walk all that distance. At about 1:30 that morning, I walked up to Sharon Slater's house with her, and her father came out on the porch again a little sterner than I wanted to see him, but with no guns. That was a relief.

"Mr. Slater," I said, "I guess you know what happened and I want to apologize for getting your daughter home so late." I should have let it go at that, but of course I went on, as I was so often prone to do. "I'm hoping you won't be mad at me because I would like to take your daughter to church in the morning and then take her out to spend tomorrow afternoon with her on a picnic with Darrell and his girl, and I promise we won't do what we did tonight. I mean what happened tonight won't happen again!"

Sharon blushed and I stammered. But her dad smiled a little. "I can see by your clothes you are telling the truth," he said. "If you want to come in and wash off some of that spare tire you have all over you, maybe it would be good to meet my wife… she has been worried sick." I did, and her mother was relieved to see that I wasn't someone she should have to worry about.

The next day we all went to church together and then went out to Carter's Lake and had a picnic and went fishing. And I know this is hard to believe, but on the way, trying to get to our destination out in the country, I tried to cross a little shallow creek and we got that old Chevy stuck right in the middle of it. I can still remember those two girls taking off their shoes and wading to the other side, while Darrell and I, stood out in the creek up to our knees in the water, jacking up the wheels of my old car, putting enough rocks under them to get out. Somehow the afternoon turned out great anyway, although Darrell wasn't in the best of moods trying to dry out his new boots. Somewhere, he has a picture of himself out there in the creek, fuming as he tried to get the jack under my submerged back bumper.

When I left that evening, so late we might not get back to

school before midnight, I was sure I might wind up coming back to Piedmont every weekend to see Sharon, and maybe settle down there with ol' Darrell as a neighbor some day. But for some stupid reason nothing ever worked out again. I think Sharon Slater went off to college shortly afterward. It must have been some college way off somewhere, too far for my bald tires to make the trip.

I am hoping she hasn't forgotten me. But truthfully it seems like it would be hard to forget someone who bungled things up as badly as I did that weekend. It is likely she told her kids about that kid from School of the Ozarks who had a car with one bad side.

Darrell Hamby with a pair of bass we caught from Table Rock Lake.

Chapter 18

HUSTLERS

Darrell Hamby and I fished all we could down on Lake Taneycomo below the School and I think it was in the winter of 1966 that tragedy struck. Dean Fry, who wasn't so much a friend of the students as Dean Todd was, sent down an edict that no student without a pass given to leave the campus, could go down over the bluff or down to the farm or off the campus after dark. He came up with a green line around the campus, which no one was suppose to cross after sunset. The reason for it was that some of the students were so romantic that I guess they wanted to sneak off in couples and listen to the sounds of the night and look at the moon and stars. Hamby and I had no problem with that, as he had his fiancé back home and I could hardly get a girl to go to the library with me, let alone sneaking off into the woods. That bluff was steep! But it created one heck of a problem for us... we fished down over that bluff on Taneycomo Lake 'til sunset, and had to clean our fish and we often didn't get back up to the campus until it was pretty dark. I went to Dr. Clark and told him that if we couldn't fish until after sunset, I would have to quit and go home. At the time, I meant it. It was hard to go to a late class, or work at a job on campus and have much time left to fish before the sun set. I told him I couldn't live without the time I spent in the woods or on the water, and Darrell and I had done a good job of supplying Dr. Clark and Dean Todd and some of the teachers some fresh trout on occasion.

He gave it some thought, talked to both deans the next day and came back with good news. He said that if it was a situation where boys were fishing on Taneycomo and no girls were involved, the School would overlook that breaking of the green line rule. Any boy who got caught coming up that steep trail from the lake after dark with a rod and reel in his hand and a stringer of trout would be okay as long as he didn't have his other arm around one of the campus coeds.

It erased the blues I was feeling in a hurry, and of course, I wondered why anyone who liked to fish as much as I did, would want to waste his time down there on that big gravel bar with a girl, as most of them I knew were not very good fishermen.

Hamby saw it as something of a miracle. He said with my connections with Dr. Clark he figured I could get my grade point raised up to a 2.4 or something like that. He said that stuff about me being the Prince of Point Lookout might not be that far off.

But let me say right here that Dr. Clark didn't only do special things for me. When he knew about any problem a student had, he tried to help. And he did, many times that I knew of, and I am sure quite often on occasions I didn't know about. Dr. Good had been the same way. Dr. Good was living on campus, getting very old, and he was one of the most beloved and honored men I have ever known. Dr. Clark thought very highly of Dr. Good, and I think they had become good friends. He had spent his time as college president before Dr. Clark, doing the things that made an education possible for big numbers of kids who could have never imagined going to school. Dr. Good and Dr. Clark were men of common sense, and when something didn't make sense, they tried to do something about it. But in doing that, they made it hard on the trout in Taneycomo, as Darrell and I wreaked havoc on 'em.

You might imagine that I was pretty good with a cue stick, since I had worked since I was eleven years old in my dad and grandfather's pool hall there in Houston, Missouri. By the time I was thirteen, I was good. I may never be as good at anything as I was at making a cue ball do what I wanted it to do. It was important to be good because sometimes it was hard for my dad to make enough money in a month to keep the place open. Every time I could get a snooker game going, and win, it was another twenty cents in the moneybag I wore that hung nearly to my knees. Being short had its advantages. I got a good look at the table without bending over much.

Hamby had been shooting pool and snooker as long as I had, and he was just as good as I was. We would take the

movie bus into Branson every now and then and instead of going to the movie, we would sneak over to the pool hall, which was right beside it. It was pretty easy to come back with ten or fifteen dollars made from some of the young guys around town who weren't nearly as good at 'nine-ball' as they thought they were. It was a gambler's game. You put nine pool balls in a diamond shaped rack on a pool table, one through nine, and the nine-ball in the center of the set.

Two or three shooters could play, even four on occasion. You flipped a coin for the shooting sequence and occasionally a good player could run the table without anyone else getting a shot. But that isn't always what you wanted to do. You put a dollar on the nine-ball, and whoever made it got a dollar from all other players. When the nine-ball went down, the game was over.

But the money was in the five-ball. You had to shoot each ball in order, but if you were shooting the deuce or trey, or four-ball, and you could sink the five-ball off that, then each player paid you another dollar and you spotted it back on the table and kept shooting. You made money by trying to make several combination shots, which sunk the five, and with those big pockets on the pool table you could re-spot it several times if you knew what you were doing. Imagine two nights in the pool hall during the week, making ten dollars in thirty minutes on occasion, when I was getting paid a dollar and thirty-five cents an hour working for Dr. Nightingale or Dr. Poole.

And then Hamby got the idea that a couple of young local smart-alecks who came in regularly and drove new cars and had lots of money might be good marks. They were snooker players, fairly good at it. I saw them take ten dollars from other players on occasion. They played Darrell one night, each one playing him a couple of games and he lost all four games and eight dollars. But what they didn't know was, he could have won all four games. He had set them up. He told them when he left he would be back in a week with more money, and they snickered a little as he left.

It wasn't hard to figure out what was going to happen. A week later we rode in on a movie bus, with all the money either one of us had, probably only twenty dollars between the two of us. I stayed in the movie lobby for a while and had some popcorn. A half hour later I walked in the pool hall and played a local fellow a game of snooker for a dollar, on the table next to where Hamby was mopping up on one of the guys who had took his money the week before. I lost badly, and I am sure they noticed that I wasn't much of a snooker player… or at least it looked that way. When the game was over, Darrell had those two guys fonchin' at the bit to get their money back. He said he guessed they could just play a three-handed game of snooker and then he looked over at me and asked if I would like to play as his partner against those two.

Darrell and I lost a couple of dollars the first game and two dollars each the second game. Then the guys wanted to play for a little more money. We each put five dollars on the table and we won the next five games. By the time we finished the last game, the bus back to S of O was gone, and Darrell and I were in a fix. Those two guys were really mad. They could figure out that I learned a great deal about shooting snooker that night in a very short time, and putting two and two together, they understood they had been hustled. It was kind of a scary situation. We took twenty-five dollars from each of them, and I guess I had never had any more than that in my pocket at one time, though there were times I had raised my bank account back in Houston to fifty or sixty dollars when working over weekends on a hay crew, or guiding float fishermen. We walked up the street a ways into the drug store and snuck out the back door and only had to walk into Hollister before we caught a ride. Late that night we climbed over the fence at the old entrance gate and got back into the dorm without getting caught.

That's the trouble with gambling on snooker games and winning a little more than someone wants to lose. You are liable to be in a tussle if the people involved are young and stupid. Hamby wasn't worried, he said he could handle both those kids all by himself and I reckon he could have. The money was tempting and he wanted to go back and see if we could take them on again, but I didn't. I told him that I could see us getting into a mess in there and it would get back to school and get both of us kicked out. It might have been the smartest decision I ever made.

Chapter 19

FOREIGNERS

Darrel Hamby and I enjoyed knowing two Japanese boys who lived in the room down the hall from us... Shuichi Araya and Takashi Watanabe. Truthfully, I never saw anyone smile as much as those two boys did. It was hard to imagine. They weren't able to go back home and see friends and family at all, and yet they seemed so happy all the time.

When you stop and think about it, there had to be a lot of prejudice in this country against Japanese people. World War II had ended only twenty years before with the atom bombs dropped on Japan. There were thousands of men in the Ozarks who were only in their forties, who had fought Japanese soldiers. And there were Ozark families who had lost sons at Pearl Harbor and in the Pacific. My mother's brother had fought in the Pacific Islands, and I knew several other World War II soldiers who came into the pool hall Dad owned. I know they had to have hated the Japanese for what they had seen and experienced.

For some reason, I never realized that back then. The two Japanese boys may have had relatives who died in the war, and some of the kids on the S of O campus may have had relatives killed by the Japanese. There we were together, the

Shuichi Araya

Takashi Watanabe

sons of deadly enemies, going to school together.

Shuichi and Takashi couldn't speak English very well and Darrell and I had a lot of fun with them. Once Darrell came back from his home in Piedmont with a big bag of venison jerky, and it was very, very good.

Shuichi and Takashi came in and sampled it and they had never tasted jerky or anything quite like it. About that time Dean Fry's big old fuzzy dog had been missing for a week or so, and everyone on campus was aware of it, as there were posters everywhere letting students know the dog was on the lam, and everyone should be looking for it. When the two Japanese boys asked what the meat was, Darrell told them it was venison. What is venison, they wanted to know... dog meat, I told them, jokingly! Darrell followed it up. "Dean Fry's dog." He said matter of factly.

They didn't get the joke. Their eyes got big, and I heard Shuichi say, "OOOH, Very bad!" They dropped the jerky and left in a hurry.

Hamby nearly rolled on the floor with laughter, but it wasn't so funny when a very stern dorm mother got wind of the rumor. Mrs. Swenty called us both down to her office and demanded an explanation. In the next day or so, the old dog found its way home, apparently from a trip to visit a girlfriend of his own somewhere. I am glad he did, because Dean Fry had absolutely no sense of humor.

We were always playing practical jokes in the dorm, and of course the two Japanese boys were perfect marks.

One warm evening in mid summer we took Shuichi snipe hunting, left him in a field to the north of the swimming pool just after dark with a sack and a stick where we told him there was a well-used snipe trail. We told him to slap the ground with the stick and hold the sack open and whistle every now and then. We told him we would go drive some snipe his way to see if we could catch one or two in his sack.

The poor kid did just what we asked, and I could kick myself today for doing it. We had no idea that there was a horse in that field, a big white one that belonged to one of the supervisors at the school. When he heard Shuichi whistling, he came trotting up the hill toward him, and it scared him half to death. He tried to jump over a barbed wire fence and tore his jeans and skinned up his arm. When we found him he was still running, his eyes as big as saucers, and all he could say was… "BIG, BIG ANIMAL…. BIG!

Darrell and I tried to apologize, but the two of us felt worthless for doing that. Who could imagine that outcome?

It made me start to realize that all jokes aren't funny for everyone, and taking responsibility for making stupid mistakes like that as part of a joke, makes a kid think a little bit how bad something might turn out. Shuichi could have been badly hurt in that stupid joke.

When we got him calmed down and explained what the snipe hunting was all about, he wasn't mad at us at all, but laughed about it himself. All I ever saw in those two boys was a gentleness and a forgiving spirit, which made you admire them.

We had some students at S of O who were absolutely humorless. They were from foreign mid-east countries like Turkey and Pakistan and Iran. They seemed to be dressed better than most of us, and they never smiled it seemed to me. It also seemed that they considered themselves to be above the Ozark kids in some way. But I noticed that some of the girls on campus really liked them, perhaps because of their neat appearance, dark skin and hair. If there were any students I found difficult to understand, they were the ones.

Sometime during that last summer, Darrell and I really got serious about the trout fishing. We would get our bait from the cafeteria... Velveeta cheese. There was an older lady there that we got to know fairly well, who served food and did all kinds of work in the kitchen. She was a delight. Sometimes on the weekend they would have sweet rolls and I loved anything sweet. If Darrell was gone, I would tell her he was back in the dorm too sick to come and eat breakfast and she would give me an extra sweet roll and a carton of milk to take to him. If I was gone, he'd do the same thing. I think she knew we were just working to get extra food, but she would just smile and shake her head and make a comment about how often Darrell was sick on a Sunday morning. Without much of an argument though, she supplied us with cheese for bait, and we would bring her some trout every now and then to take home.

We began to have some competition on the gravel bar though, as Mark McWorthless and a couple of his ratty friends would come down and try to catch trout. One of the guys kept pestering Darrell to give him the low-down on any special bait he might be using. Hamby got so good at catching trout that they figured he had to be using a special bait.

On that steep, winding trail that led down over the bluff to the gravel bar that summer, there was a rock ledge about head high you had to work around because of a big red wasp nest. They aren't so feisty in the early summer, but about mid-August those wasps got mean, and they would sting anyone who got close.

Darrell finally told one of the three that we had been having awfully good luck on trout using wasp larva from a couple of wasp nests found in the tool shed at Dr. Clark's home, and now we were running short of bait so we were going to have to figure out a way to get that nest along the bluff trail.

It was gone soon after, and I took a strange delight in the swollen eye of McWorthless, who somehow had got stung several times by red wasps. Only Hamby could have come up with something like that.

We kept in touch with each other for most of the years after we left School, and when we were both married and raising kids we would even get our families together once and awhile at the lake. As this book was being finished, we planned a future float trip on the St. Francis River over near Patterson, Missouri where Darrell grew up and still lives. And while I am there we may go by the local pool hall and see if we can hustle somebody.

Chapter 20

THE BIG BASS

When it came to fishing, Darrell Hamby had more experience than I did, I have to give him that. But he was a couple of years older than me, so there's the reason behind the edge he had. I told him I started fishing when I was six. To which he replied that he started fishing when he was five. That means if he was telling the truth and I was telling the truth, he actually had three years of experience on me. However since I was lying completely, I figure he was too.

I came to School of the Ozarks College thinking it was the end of fishing and hunting for a while. Back in Houston High School, real smart kids didn't hunt and fish much, they studied. But if you have the tendency to hunt and fish and forget the books, it is a hard thing to overcome. When I stood on the point there at S of O and looked down on Lake Taneycomo, with Table Rock Lake barely showing on the horizon, I figured the Good Lord was telling me that fishing was just as important as studying.

Hamby felt that way too. I met him on the gravel bar down below the school, there on Lake Taneycomo. You had to work to get to that gravel bar. The path leading to it from the campus was down a steep bluff, and if you stepped in the wrong place you could endure a fall of significant consequences. But going down it was nothing like going up it. If you had a limit of trout thrown over your shoulder, you needed to be fit to gain the level ground on top of that ridge, something like a United States Marine after boot camp.

Back home on the Piney River in Texas County, I fished with braided line on old Shakespeare and Pflueger casting reels, using a couple of feet of monofilament leader. I could tell that this Hamby kid knew nothing about fishing, because he had one of those open-faced spinning reels, a sissified outfit if I ever saw one. But try as I might, I couldn't cast a lure out as far as he could.

And shucks, he wasn't even fishing with a shimmy-fly or a flatfish or a midget-didget, he was fishing with cheese! What kind of nitwit fishes with cheese, I asked myself? That evening in June, there on the gravel bar where the cold flowing water of Taneycomo swirled and swept past us, I learned what just two years of extra experience could teach a kid. I didn't think there was a chance anyone close to my age was as good a fisherman as me, and the first one I come across since being gone from home only one week ... was! Then I found out he'd been there at S of O for a year before I got there. No wonder he knew so much.

With that kind of experience behind him, Darrell knew all about trout fishing, and he showed me how to fish for trout. I was accustomed to catching smallmouth and goggle-eye. I hadn't even seen a trout before. Hamby told me you ate them with the scales on! Who ever heard of such a thing? He had a little frying pan and a hot plate hidden in his dorm room, and we became good friends on account of he needed me ... as a fish-eater. He needed several fish-eaters, especially one who couldn't catch them

as easily as he could. We'd go fishing that first summer and he'd catch his limit and part of mine. For Hamby, it was almost as good as finding a friend who had lots of money.

There are many good stories about those two years of trout fishing there at S of O, and fishing adventures over on Table Rock, but this isn't one of them. Because in time, Darrell and I started going fishing over in his area, near Piedmont, Missouri, when we had weekends free. At first we made the long trip in that old banged-up '54 Chevy of mine. Somehow that old car got us halfway across southern Missouri, to fish places Hamby knew best.

Finally I told him I would show him God's country, the Big Piney River where I had grown up. And that's where we caught the big one, a largemouth bass bigger than I had ever seen.

We drove to my folks' place on a Friday afternoon from S of O and we borrowed my dad's pick-up, which was old and beat up a whole lot like my car, and drove down over some private land that one of my former teachers owned, to a beautiful spot on the south side of the river, where Hog Creek flowed into the Piney. On Friday afternoon, we unloaded my wooden johnboat, which Dad had built, and set up a canvas lean-to where we would sleep in old musty camping blankets I had used for years on a hundred different gravel bars. Lightweight tents and sleeping bags had been invented by then, but I wasn't quite rich enough to own them.

On the river that evening, we were anticipating a nice stringer of goggle-eye. When darkness came we were sitting on the bank with a bucket of night crawlers and a nice campfire, and the goggle-eye were hungry. Goggle-eye or rock bass, feed better at night than they do in the daytime, it seems, and it wasn't long until we had a nice stringer of the bantam weight panfish.

The next morning we were up early trying to catch some brown bass on topwater lures, and by noon we were seining doughgut minnows and chubs on a nearby shoal to use as bait on a trotline. That Saturday evening we had trotline set and baited by the time the sun settled under the treetops upriver. The water was deep there, the line only a few feet away from a big flat boulder, which rose up out of the depths a few feet from the bank. It was a place Grandpa and Dad always called 'catfish rock', a long hole and a short shoal above our campsite. Just a few weeks before, when redbud trees were beginning to bloom, Alvin Barton and I had caught a thirty-pound flathead catfish from the depths beside it. I told Hamby that I expected a bigger one, that night in late May.

The big catfish which Alvin Barton and I had taken from the River the week before. You can see in my t-shirt my devotion to School of the Ozarks.

Half worn out, the two of us wrapped up in those blankets just after dark, and dozed off as the campfire embers waned, and wood smoke settled across the river valley there at the mouth of Hog Creek. A chuck-wills-widow serenaded us from the hillside across the creek, and barred owls called from down the river. There was no moonlight, and I had an idea that big catfish would prowl that night.

At first light, we paddled my old green johnboat, wet with dew, up the quiet river to our trotline. I knew we'd have a catfish, and we did. I could feel him when I picked up the line, lunging against the staging which had him hooked solid. But we had more than just a catfish, we had a big old soft shell turtle too. The catfish was five or six pounds and the turtle was probably twice as heavy. Both would be good eating, but they were a long ways from what we were hoping for. We were wanting a flathead so big that he would feed one big family for a week.

At mid-stream, a good fifteen feet from catfish rock, it was apparent there was nothing else to look forward to on that line. It hung limp in my hand. I pulled along it anyway, toward the far bank, expecting nothing. But then there was a slight tug, and I saw a flash of green ahead, a few feet beneath the surface. This was no catfish; it was a huge largemouth bass, bigger than any I had ever caught from the river. He was alive, but not fighting much. He was nearly done in, and when I hoisted him into the boat it was apparent that he wasn't going to survive. That big number 06 hook had lodged in one of his gills as he swallowed the chub we had baited it with. He was a big beautiful bass, about to cash in, and we both thought the same thing at once. But Darrell said it first ... "Bass season don't open until next week!" he muttered.

I was in college with one goal, to someday be a game warden on the Big Piney River, just like my old friend Bland Wilson. I had darn near got my Grandpa and Dad talked into living by most all the game laws and I just couldn't break the law myself or I would look like a hypocritiac, or whatever it was you were when you preached one thing and practiced another.

I was trying my best to be a good conservationist, which sort of went against my ancestral genetics. Hamby's ancestral genetics were even worse than mine. His idea of a chess game was outsmarting a game warden. And there wasn't any ambition in either of us to put a dying fish back in the water to be eaten by turtles, especially if it was six or seven pounds.

That Sunday morning, while folks back in my old church there in Houston were singing "I'll Fly Away" and "Shall We Gather at the River", and Reverend Morton was preaching against lyin' and cheatin' and stealin', Darrell and I were loading the truck at breakneck speed, trying to get that illegal bass back to my folks' place. We had come up with a heck of a plan. Should a game warden apprehend us, we would say we caught the bass from my Uncle Roy's farm pond. Bass were legal when taken from lakes or farm ponds, it was just rivers where they were not allowed until the last weekend of May.

Uncle Roy had a dandy bass pond. But he lived on the opposite end of the county. I knew, after he got out of church, he'd back us up if need be. Sometimes Uncle Roy would sleep through the sermon just like I had so many times and while neither of us would have come right out and lied on a Sunday, there were lots of ways to tell the truth.

Knowing my whole career hung in the balance, I was as nervous as a hen-house possum. It would kill me if Ron Roellig, the local conservation agent who had taken Bland Wilson's old job, found out I was a low-down violator. But then again, I figured the good Lord didn't want someone to waste a magnificent fish that had so much meat on it. Hamby volunteered to do the talking just in case. He said he had talked to a lot of game wardens and it was a fine art.

We drove that old pick-up toward home, with a johnboat sticking out the back of it, and water sloshing out of the metal Coleman cooler where we had the bass, which was now dead. At the edge of town, there were red lights flashing ahead of us and I darned near had a pulmonary tribulation. But it was the local police car at the site of a fender bender, which had that secondary road closed, which we needed to take to my folks' home out west of town. There was no choice but to go right down Main Street, right through the middle of town.

I never realized that Ron Roellig went to church, but that Sunday one of those big "First Something" churches was getting out, and there he was, with his wife, all dressed up and crossing the street right in front of us. He waved and I floor-boarded it. No one ever turned the corner at the Bank of Houston and McKnight's Drugstore quite as fast as I did that Sunday at ten minutes past noon. Thankfully the town's only policeman was tied up with that fender bender a mile away and the game warden had on a coat and tie and was carrying a bible. All Darrell and I had to do was make it to Dad's cellar and lock it behind us 'til the evidence was destroyed.

Hamby said later that I was the last person he'd ever partner with if he wanted to rob a bank or steal somebody's hubcaps. Truthfully, I just never was made for breaking the law or being calm in a pinch.

Before we went back to college that evening, we ate some of that bass, and Dad said we had done awful good not to let him go to waste. Mom got out the Polaroid and took a photo of the two us in the cellar with that old dead bass, and later Darrell told somebody he caught it on his fly rod.

It was mid-week before I relaxed a little, and about midsummer I went to Ron Roellig and spilled the beans. I told him I wasn't fit to be a game warden and might have to aim my sights lower. Maybe I would be a lawyer or something like that.

Ron smiled and said he was awfully glad he didn't float the river that morning where he would have had to catch me and confiscate that big fish. But he said he too would have had a hard time releasing a bass like that to be eaten by turtles. Neither one of us much admired those doggone hard-shell turtles. He said he didn't think he needed to write me a citation, since I had owned up to it and was repentful like I was. He wanted to know who I was fishing with, but I wouldn't tell him. I said I would as soon take all the blame myself, and besides that if I were to tell him who was with me, my partner would likely choke me to death, being older and more experienced than me.

I never did get to be a game warden. I think it was the Good Lord punishing me for keeping that bass, or maybe for skipping church so many Sunday mornings to go fishing or hunting. Why he never seemed to punish Darrell Hamby I do not know. That lucky cuss just kept catching fish like it was an art, or a gift. Maybe the Good Lord takes into account the fact that Hamby always has had a couple more years of experience, even to this very day.

The big bass that Darrell and I caught illegally from the Big Piney a couple of weeks before bass season opened. The photo was taken from the safe confines of my dad's cellar.

A view of Clevenger Cove in 1968, a year after I went off to Missouri University. The old v-bottomed aluminum boat the School kept chained to a tree was still there. It was that boat which we used to catch so many bass from the lake, every chance we got.

Chapter 21

PETER ENGLER & STEVE MILLER

While I was at School of the Ozarks, I had access to that aluminum lake boat at Clevenger Cove, which was owned by the School of the Ozarks at that time. Darrell Hamby and I stayed there often in the old house that must have been built in the 1800's. The boat had no motor but I paddled it all over that part of the lake when it wasn't too windy, and

I picked up a couple of pretty pieces of driftwood which I gave my mother. One of her friends worked in a flower shop and she told mom that if I could get her a dozen of those sun-bleached little stumps she would give me a dollar apiece for them.

It wasn't long after that when I took my old car over to the lake, paddled up in a cove and picked up a whole boatful of them. None were the same, and they were beautiful. I showed them to a florist in Branson and she told me that she couldn't use them, but I should show them to a fellow at Silver Dollar City by the name of Peter Engler, who was the best woodcarver in the whole country.

He was too! When I went to see him I took a couple of my sample driftwood pieces in to his woodcarving shop. Silver Dollar City was much different then, but attracting thousands of tourists, and my jaw dropped open when I saw what Peter Engler created. His carvings were magnificent. I introduced myself and figured he might laugh at me for what I was trying to do, but not Peter. He was one of the nicest men I have ever met, and he didn't laugh. He told me that he really liked the wood, and if I would get him some nice pieces he could do more carving and not do so much searching for pieces to carve.

We really hit it off, and as a kid who never had enough money to pay for everything, the driftwood and Mr. Engler made a great difference.

My old '54 Chevy that my grandfather had owned was about on its last legs, so with that trunkful of driftwood stumps, I made fifty dollars that day. With that money I went back to the junkyard in Houston, and bought a 1956 Oldsmobile. It probably was worth more than that for parts, but it really ran good, and the radio worked and it had a

Peter Engler

trunk twice the size of the old Chevy. While I had to buy a 30-cent can of oil about every two hundred miles for the old '54 Chevy, I could go almost 500 miles with that Oldsmobile before it needed oil. And I know it is hard to believe but that blue and white '56 Olds, which didn't have any rust or dents in it, had electric seats which went up and down or back and forth just by hitting a button on the side

That feature scared the dickens out of a girl I took to the drive-in once. She kept saying it seemed as if the seat was moving! It also had an automatic light dimmer, which sat on the dash on the left side and dimmed the lights when it picked up an oncoming set of car lights.

With that car and a small outboard motor I borrowed from Dave Barker, the campus landscaping boss, I could go out in the lake farther, and I took Peter Engler load after load of beautiful driftwood from Table Rock Lake. We got to be good friends and he told me he would teach me to carve someday when I had time. Then he asked me where I was getting all that beautiful wood and I got to thinking he might hire someone else to go get it. So I told him we were diving for it, and then drying it in the sun, a lengthy process which was time consuming and costly. He grinned at me and said I surely must be a good diver! Peter knew all about finding that driftwood, but he also knew how poor School of the Ozarks' students were, and he did his best to help me.

When I would offer him a really nice stump and tell him I needed two dollars for it, he would tell me it was easily worth three dollars, and pay me that much. But he would take one of those stumps and turn it into one of the most beautiful pieces of art I have ever seen, and sell it for a hundred dollars. This was about the time that I was finishing my two years at School of the Ozarks and when I left, I still went back to get a load of driftwood on occasion.

When I came back to work as a park naturalist that summer on Table Rock Lake, I kept taking driftwood to Peter Engler. He and I became good friends, and he helped me save a lot of money to pay the bills at the University of Missouri after I left S of O.

A few years back, about 2009 I think it was, I was delivering some of my books to a bookstore in the Grand Village Shopping Center at Branson, and there was a big woodcarving shop with Peter Engler's name on it. I found him there, carving a piece of wood and I walked up and asked him if he'd like to buy some driftwood retrieved from the depths of Table Rock Lake by an accomplished diver? He smiled again, like he did the first time I met him, and shook my hand. He was growing old, but he remembered me and I couldn't believe it. I left him some of the magazines I was publishing and all of my books. We talked for a long time, and I left there with my spirits lifted.

Peter Engler had used his shop at Silver Dollar City and that one in the Grand Village Mall to help many woodcarvers get started and have a place to sell their work. I went back a couple of years later and they told me he had just recently passed away. If men who are gentle and kind and men who help others as much as they can have a place in heaven, Peter Engler is there. If great artists gather there to keep creating wondrous things, then God certainly is pleased with him.

At S of O, I tried to carve a little and gave it up. I tried to paint wildlife and the results looked awful. Once I painted a fish and framed it and gave it to a girlfriend back in Houston. I don't suppose she liked it much because in a month or so she gave it back to me because she found a boyfriend who had a brand new car. I guess she wasn't impressed with those electric seats in my Oldsmobile.

I met another artist who really impressed me. He could paint beautiful scenes, wildlife and people, and he wrote some beautiful poetry. I have already mentioned Steve Miller, the curator of the School of the Ozarks Museum.

As I said in another chapter, I was pretty good at fixing old guns, and I could carve out gunstocks too in Dr. Clark's workshop. Mr. Miller gave me several to fix and I made a couple of stocks for old muzzle-loaders that had none. He got to talking to me about my future. We sat down one day

One of the gunstocks I made for the museum and Steve Miller. The band around the forestock near my thumb was temporary until a screw that fit there could be made in the machine shop. I loved working on guns, but when you figured up what I made with the hours I put into that stock, I probably didn't make much.

and he told me that he was a friend of Mr. Mottesheard, the conservation teacher, a man who had retired from the Missouri Conservation Commission.

He said that Mottie, as everyone called him, had been impressed with my interest in the outdoors, and he felt I needed to transfer to the University of Missouri at Columbia to major in wildlife management and get the classes I needed that School of the Ozarks didn't have. I asked if I thought that would help me in my quest to be a game warden, and he pointed out that I might even want to aim higher than that.

I nearly blew everything one April night in 1966 when Jay Johnson and Dane Allen and I went back home to spend the weekend on the Big Piney River where I grew up. We put my old boat in on a Friday evening, floated downstream for about thirty minutes and set up our camp on a gravel bar. We brought with us some bass and trout caught on Table Rock and Taneycomo, and were about to fry them when a canoe came slipping down the river, with a game warden I knew well, Ron Roellig. This was back in a time when conservation agents worked miles away from their pick-ups and worked alone.

Today they always work in pairs and they do not get out far from their vehicles. Times were different then, and the Conservation Department in Missouri was a far cry from what it is today, an agency you could respect and see working for the good of outdoorsmen and natural resources. All I wanted to be then was a conservation agent, hoping my college education would help me land that job.

I was glad to see Ron, he checked our fishing licenses and I cheerfully asked him to sit down and join us in a fish fry, telling him we had more bass and trout than we could eat.

He was quiet and somber, and then he asked me why I had those bass. Then it hit me… bass were legal on Table Rock, but not on the Big Piney. I told him what we had done, and how I had never thought about the illegality of bringing them to the river. I explained they had been caught on Table Rock and I told him Mr. Mottesheard would vouch for me if he would only call him.

Mr. Roellig gave it some thought, and he could see that a couple of the bass were still about half frozen. He also could see that we had trout, which couldn't have come from the river, as the Big Piney didn't have any trout. He said he was going to let me go pending a call to Mr. Mottesheard at S of O. He said he knew Mottie well.

My knees were weak as Ron Roellig floated on down the river, and he told me as I went to eat all those bass and not take any with me. We did. The next week Mr. Mottesheard saw me on campus and with a big grin, said he heard I had been confused about the difference between lake rules and river rules. Later he told me he had assured Ron Roellig that I was just a kid who caught way too many fish, and that I should be watched every time I came home to float the Piney.

Steve Miller heard about what I had done, and he ribbed me about it. He said that a convicted violator likely would have had a hard time transferring to a major university to study to be a game warden.

Of course I had no idea what it took to get in at MU, and my grade point was under 2.5. Today, no student with a grade point that low could transfer to a major university, though a low grade point wouldn't interfere with being a modern conservation agent. In the last semester of my second year at S of O, Steve Miller must have pulled some strings. He called me over to the museum and told me I had been accepted at the University and he told me he had paper work he would help me fill out. Of course, once again, I was apprehensive, as I had been when I graduated from high school and the guidance counselor helped me apply to S of O. Fortunately, all the classes I had taken over the past two years would transfer except one... an old testament class under Dr. Stone. Ironically, that was one of the best classes I took, because I learned so much about Bible history.

I didn't really want to go to the University of Missouri but Steve Miller told me I needed to do it, to recognize the potential he felt I had. What potential, I thought... no one knew what a goof up and failure I really was. I had gotten by because I had fooled a lot of teachers and learned a little about being a young con artist. I was no scholar. I told him I just didn't have the money to pay the tuition and dormitory costs anywhere, and he reminded me that I hadn't had any money when I came to School of the Ozarks. "You can work there just like you worked here," he told me. "The School will give you a campus job in the archaeology department, fifteen hours a week. They will pay you well, and you can apply for some Federal funds."

I never did apply for any financial help, but during the last semester of my schooling there, they called me in and told me they new about my work off campus at the pool hall in Columbia, and told me they could give me a thousand dollars in a government grant if I would agree not to work off campus. I agreed, and boy did that ever help my studies. That semester I think my grade point soared to an all time high of 2.6 or thereabouts. At the end of my second year out of college, I returned the thousand dollars to the financial office of M.U. but never heard anything from them. It was a matter of pride. As poor as we had been, none of my family or any of my grandparents had ever had government assistance of any kind. I didn't want to be the first.

Steve Miller was a man I respected greatly. He was not only a fine artist, he was a great writer. Years after he had died, I published a book entitled Rivers to Run. On the back cover, I used part of a poem he had written, over a photo of two old wooden johnboats sitting on the Buffalo River one winter morning. The poem read, "I'm an old johnboat, born to float, I ran as the river flowed. And got my rest on gravel bars where campfire embers glowed".

One of the most talented people I met at School of the Ozarks, Steve Miller.

I owe a lot to Steve Miller. Mostly because of him, I was walking around the campus of the University of Missouri

Steve Miller was quite interested in Ozark bluff dwellers from thousands of years ago, and he did this painting of what he imagined life would have been like in that time.

in the fall of 1967, with my jaw dropped open, looking at the mammoth library, the huge dormitories and a student union big enough to hold the entire population at Point Lookout. They told me I was on probation. If I didn't make a 2.5 grade average that first semester, I was gone. And by golly, even though I was working at two jobs about thirty hours a week, I made it. Every other semester I was on probation, but I always got through. Looking back, it was nothing short of a miracle that I didn't flunk out. I came awfully close when an algebra teacher took pity on me and helped me make a D in her class with extra work.

But I couldn't grasp it. Algebra and higher mathematics like Trigonometry were so difficult for me that I never ever could figure anything out. But writing, and natural science courses were so easy for me. I remember telling that algebra teacher that I would never use algebra, I just wanted to be a game warden someday. No game or fish limits I knew of amounted to more than ten. If x equaled ten and some fishermen had x minus 5 bass, I could easily figure that out!!!

In January of 1970, I received a B.S. degree in wildlife management from the University of Missouri and got a diploma, which I still have. In all the years since, no one ever asked to see it. But I got that diploma because of School of the Ozarks and the foundation it gave me. In the two and a half years I spent at the University of Missouri, I never asked for any financial assistance, and I am proud that I found an off-campus job at a pool hall, which helped me pay my school costs. It was that work ethic that I found at School of the Ozarks, which made all that work. But today I realize that I would never have taken that leap, leaving the place where I loved to be, going off to a school where I became only a number, 133746, if it had not been for a lot of great people I have written about in these pages.

Chapter 22

LANE DAVIS

While at School of the Ozarks, I was fortunate enough to begin writing my first real outdoor column. In my hometown of Houston, Missouri, the editor of the Houston Herald newspaper was a fellow by the name of Lane Davis. While I was a kid back in high school, guiding fishermen on weekends, Lane and his son Robert were regular clients of mine. They liked to float the Big Piney, the Little Piney and the Roubidoux.

I didn't have to offer Lane any advice, he was a good fisherman. All he needed of me was to paddle the boat and see to it he was the right casting distance from the best fishing water. While he didn't need my advice, I gave him quite a bit. At fourteen or fifteen years of age, I just couldn't keep my mouth shut and paddle. I told him often that if he would leave that aluminum johnboat at home and use our wooden ones, he would catch more fish, and I was quick to point out that whatever lure he was using wasn't as good, in my opinion, as a flatfish or a midget-didget, or even a shimmy-fly for that matter. Lane was a kind man who just smiled and argued with me on a good-natured keel, never once telling me to shut up and paddle, like some of my city clients did.

I went back home one spring weekend and Lane called to

tell me he needed a guide. I told him I was getting 75 cents an hour since I had begun college, instead of the 50 cents an hour I charged while in high school. Lane always gave me a five-dollar tip for a day of fishing, so it didn't make much difference. He said he would pay me the increased hourly fee, and just take it out of the tip. I never did excel in mathematics, so I thought I came out ahead on the deal.

On the river that day I told him I had given up on being a game warden and intended to be an outdoor writer like Jack O'Connor and Ben East. That day we worked out a deal wherein I would write a weekly column for the Herald, entitled "Summer on the Piney". In the fall we would change the title to "Fall on the Piney," and then "Winter on the Piney" and so forth.

He told me I knew as much about the Big Piney River and its fish and wild creatures as anyone he ever knew at my age. That was quite a compliment, from a man who had fished with my grandfather and my dad and uncle. But it was then he added something… "You have everything in the world to learn about writing." No truer words were ever spoken, and there were few men who could have done as good a job at teaching me than Lane. Or should I say… there were few who could have taught me as efficiently as he. Sometimes there are different ways of saying the same thing. Growing up in that pool hall as a kid always caused me to write as I would talk. I don't think Hemingway did that.

To tell the truth, if it hadn't been for that day, I don't know if I would have ever had any success as a newspaper columnist. A couple of years later, upon transferring to the University of Missouri, I went to the Columbia Missourian newspaper and talked them into letting me write a weekly outdoor column for them. There were two newspapers there in Columbia at the time and the other one had an outdoor column. The Missourian didn't, and when they saw those copies of my column, torn from the Houston Herald, they called and talked with Lane Davis. The next thing I knew I was writing a weekly column for them, and receiving ten dollars for each one. I don't know what Lane Davis told them, but he surely was the influencing factor.

I will never forget the time when I trudged over to the Library at School of the Ozarks, upset because Lake Taneycomo was so overrun with boats and people and houses being built everywhere along its banks. Our dormitory mother, Mrs. Swenty, was married to the S of O postmaster, and they were both great people. But her husband had bought a little tract of land on Taneycomo just upstream from the bridge that crossed the river from Branson to Hollister. Since I was always looking for work, he hired me and two other boys from the dorm to work one weekend digging a septic tank hole for the little cottage he intended to build only a stone's throw from the river. The ground was nothing but sand, and we dug a deep wide hole there next to the river in one weekend. Then we started digging septic lines between the tank and the water. We joked about how he might as well just dig a line to Lake Taneycomo and dump his sewage into the lake, that's how inefficient that sewage system in the sand would be.

That week I wrote my weekly column about the development and the overflow of people created by the building of Table Rock Dam, and talked about how the White River had been a great natural stream, something special in the Ozarks, and how we had destroyed it forever in the name of progress and money. Lane ran the column and never changed a word. Several small newspapers picked up the column and Branson was one of them. The next week the Houston Herald ran a letter on the same page as my column, from a very indignant businessman in Branson. He pointed out in a very satirical matter that while the hoot owls liked the White the way it used to be, the people who had lived there in poverty for so long preferred the progress and a better way of life the dam offered everyone due to the economic lift of tourism, more people, more boats and bright lights.

I was intent upon writing another column answering his letter, letting my readers hear another side, and pointing out that over-development was the result of greed, and money didn't necessarily mean happiness, and that if it did, it shouldn't.

Lane told me to send another column, and I was indignant. I wanted to answer the guy. We sat down in his office, and he told me some things I have never forgotten in all my years as a writer.

"You are supposed to be a professional," he said, "a newspaper columnist. You don't get into an argument with your column, never use it as some way to spar with someone who doesn't agree with what you wrote. You had the opportunity to put your convictions on a subject out there for the world to read. It is your first and last word, and if others want to contest it...that is what newspapers are all about. As long as his argument is reasonable and respectful and his opinion reflects another side of an issue, he deserves an opportunity to be published in our readers' section. Let readers decide if your points are strong."

Lane could see I was awfully disappointed, so he slapped me on the back and told me to keep writing. "You made a passionate and reasonable plea for your side of the story, and lots of folks agreed with you. Lots of folks didn't. That's the way it is with journalism. If you intend to make a difference in the world as a conservationist and naturalist, you've got to develop some pretty thick skin."

Then he said something I have always remembered. "Figure out what you believe is right and pursue it. Stick to your convictions! But give those who don't agree with you a chance to have their say, and don't get bruised up by it. When readers see that you can listen to the other side, they will pay a great deal of attention to what you write."

I took several writing courses at School of the Ozarks over the next couple of years, and I never did make very good grades in those courses. I don't know whatever made me think I could make a living as a writer after those grades I got. Maybe part of it was an old editor back on the Piney River, cheering me on, and telling me I could do it, and teaching me about what a writer should be.

Townsend Godsey was the S of O student newspaper sponsor and a journalism instructor who was an accomplished writer.

Chapter 23

TOWNSEND GODSEY

Townsend Godsey was the journalism instructor at School of the Ozarks and a good writer with many magazine articles to his credit and one of the best books written about School of the Ozarks, which is titled, "The Flight of the Phoenix." It is a tremendous book, and everyone who has any interest in the School, now called the College of the Ozarks, and its philosophy and history, should read the book. Even today, when I go back through old magazines I occasionally find his byline, and that of his good friend Dan Saults.

Mr. Godsey knew I was writing an outdoor column for my hometown paper, The Houston Herald, and he gave me the opportunity to write an outdoor column in the little School newspaper at S of O. Only recently I came across some of them, and they made me wince. I should have waited until I got older to write a column... much older.

While I don't really think Mr. Godsey had much faith in my writing ability, as illustrated in the journalism and writing grades he gave me, he helped me tremendously by showing me how to prepare a manuscript for sale to a magazine. I used that knowledge to sell some stories to a little magazine in Texas called "All Outdoors". Those stories made me 35 dollars each, and I couldn't believe it when I got those checks.

I owe Mr. Godsey much. When I went to the University of Missouri as a junior, I used him for a reference to get a weekly column with the Columbia Missourian newspaper and they told me he had been contacted and gave me a good recommendation. That was a big step for me. I think that Townsend Godsey also helped me to get into a journalism class at Missouri University.

I was majoring in wildlife management, in the School of Agriculture. Journalism classes were for what they called J-School students, and they and the instructors were some of the snootiest people I ever ran into. I got into a J-School feature writing class against the instructors wishes and I never ever wrote a paper that didn't get me a 'D' grade. Here I was writing an outdoor column for the local Columbia newspaper for ten dollars a week, and he really didn't like that much. My features for his class were always about the outdoors of course, and I sold a couple of them to All Outdoors magazine down in Texas. They would use them as I wrote them, and the journalism instructor would cut them all to pieces. Finally I asked him why. Here I am helping to pay my college bills by writing and selling my stuff, and he's giving me D's.

He was sort of a stuffed shirt and I didn't like him much, but I have to admit he gave me good advice. He told me that his Journalism School within the University of Missouri was one of the most prestigious in all the world. He asked me if I realized that Tennessee Williams had come from the MU Journalism School. It didn't help much that I didn't know who the heck Tennessee Williams was, nor any of the other big shot writers he named who he had personally known.

I knew Jack London and Mark Twain and Zane Grey hadn't gone there!

He told me in frustration that he was never going to give me anything but a D on anything I wrote, because he didn't much like for some hillbilly kid out of the School of Agriculture to weasel his way into his prestigious and renowned Journalism Classes.

Then came the good advice... "In my class there are young men and women who will become professionals, working for the biggest newspapers in the nation as columnists and editors. Why don't you just forget trying to compete with them, drop this class and do your own thing as best you can and see where it gets you."

I did. Two years later I took a job as an outdoor editor and columnist for the Arkansas Democrat, that state's largest daily newspaper. That same year I began writing for Outdoor Life magazine, and shortly after that, Field and Stream, national magazines with millions of readers. Before I turned twenty-five one of those magazine features I had written was published in a book of sports stories published in New York entitled, "Best Sport Stories of 1972". My article, entitled, "Old Paint" was the story of an old wooden johnboat I had grown up with on the Big Piney River, and it is part of the first book of short stories I published years ago.

I don't say any of this in a boastful way. I have never been a writer, I am just someone who puts things down on paper the way I learned to do it, much the same way I would tell a story if I was speaking it. Of course I have been lucky. But anything I have accomplished in my life has little to do with talent, more to do with determination and hard work, and the help of God. I ask for that help constantly.

It has to do to with having faith, having confidence, and listening to all who try to teach you, as Townsend Godsey did me. If you are someone who wants to accomplish something you feel your Creator meant for you to do, go at it with a bulldog determination. Never get too proud, but never be ashamed of who and what you are. And cast aside the discouragement you can get from those who say you can't do it, and hope you will fail. Ignore them.

I say this of course to young people today when I speak to school groups around the Midwest. I tell them to follow their passion, which is usually where their talents and gifts are found. Do not listen for a moment to those who tell you to go into this field or hat because that is where the money is. I say something similar to older folks when I speak to church groups, retirement groups, and civic clubs and organizations. You are never too old to get the heck out of what you are discontent with and tackle something you always wanted to do.

Things work out, it seems, for those who have a passion to do something they love. How many hundreds of times was I told that I should forget free-lance writing because I could never make enough money to support a family? Somehow, God helped me to have what I needed, always, even if I never achieved wealth. I always figured that if I could be happier paddling a johnboat down the river than I could be in a yacht, it is sort of crazy to work my life away to buy a yacht. No one is happier than someone who figures out what he was put here on earth to do, money or no money. And you are never too old to turn that direction.

I'll tell you what it takes to be a writer... a pen and a notebook.

Chapter 24

REUBEN

I couldn't write the account of my experience during those two years at School of the Ozarks without adding this one chapter in a very serious tone. One summer Saturday I went with a group of young men who worked on the School of the Ozarks' farm to buck bales of hay in a field across Lake Taneycomo. I suppose it was a piece of ground the school owned, and I was there to work off the debt I owed Dean Todd for ruining Bob Carr's pillow and mattress with an egg. I had spent years bucking bales back home on the watershed of the Big Piney, and I actually enjoyed it. Our crew that day had the first black person I had ever met or talked to... I will call him Reuben.

There are many reasons I will remember Reuben. He became my friend, and taught me a great deal of what I know about black people and what we today refer to as racism. In the first place, Reuben's skin was not black, it was just brown. And my skin was a long way from white, it was sort of a mixture between tan and red, depending on which part of me you were talking about. It seemed stupid to refer to him as black and me as white, so as I remember it, we never did. I am not going to call the dark-skinned men I have met since as Negro or African-American or colored. If I did that, I feel that I would have to refer to myself as Caucasian, French-Indian-Scotch-Irish American, or uncolored. Reuben was a dark-skinned friend of mine. Over the years I have had many friends who had darker skin than I. Certainly the most of them descended from slaves brought over from distant lands.

I myself descended from a primitive Canadian Cree Indian woman and a French boy who was a stowaway on a ship, running from the law in his native country. On my mother's side were the drinkin'est, fightin'est Scotch Irish immigrants who ever came overseas. No man should be ashamed of his ancestry, as he can't change it. We are today what we make ourselves, not what our ancestors were.

With a couple of the dark-skinned men I got to know well, I broached the question... "Have you ever thought, that as awful as slavery was, that it has made life for you much better than if your ancestors had stayed in their native land?" Their answers have been varied. But most realize that slavery began with the selling of people from Africa to slave traders by people who were much like them... dark skinned native tribesmen who raided other villages and took captives. It began that way, and got much worse. I cannot imagine a place in heaven for those who were involved in that, or for those slave-owners who were cruel and tortuous people to members of those people forced into slavery. And I also realize there were slave-owners who were kind and considerate of those people who worked for them.

There is little doubt that some southern plantation owners treated slaves very well, and actually became close friends with many of them. But the cruelty of some others was horrible.

Whatever that situation was, my ancestors owned no

slaves, and they lived as poor as any dark skinned people living in destitution on southern plantations. My father, as a boy lived in a cabin on the river that had dirt floors, and an old barrel for a stove. He and his brothers slept on homemade mattresses stuffed with duck feathers and leaves when they were boys.

I knew nothing of dark skinned people when I was young. The old guys in the pool hall that I grew up around weren't people filled with hate. They referred to dark skinned people as 'colored', or 'darkeys' and neither term was meant to be insulting. There were a couple who referred to dark skinned men in insulting terms, and you could tell they hated them. But my dad stepped in to let me know when I was young that he felt God looked at all of us the same, and if you hated any men, you were going to be found wanting when you someday stood in judgment after you died.

I well remember what he told me when I was about ten or twelve years old... He said, "I met dark skinned people in St. Louis when I went there to work when I was only fifteen years old, not much older than you. There were many of them that were despicable people and I stayed away from them."

Then I remember him shifting his pipe in his mouth and looking at me to make a strong point... "But there were more of them that I liked," he said, "they were just ordinary folks with their own way of doing things, and quite a bit different than me. But still they were good people, and a few of them I was proud to call my friends."

How anyone could have disliked Reuben is beyond me. At School of the Ozarks, he made a lot of friends, but I can't remember if there was anyone of his race attending school there at the time. He was soft-spoken and quiet, almost shy. But there was always a smile on his face, as if he knew something funny that you didn't. We worked together that whole day bucking bales on the farm, and by the time we returned to S of O, there was nothing uncomfortable between us. We talked about the things I always wanted to know and didn't understand. Both of us being so poor made it easier, I suppose. But I liked everything about him. At first it seemed he was just like me. At first!!

But Reuben grew up in Pine Bluff, Arkansas and there wasn't much about Pine Bluff that was like the little town of Houston, Mo. Reuben liked a lot different kind of music than me and he liked dancing. I didn't know a thing about dancing and didn't want to learn. I thought dancing was really embarrassing, I couldn't see myself doing that.

And he had something I would have loved to have, but had never had… a girlfriend who loved him, and he loved her. Knowing how close they were, I don't know how he stayed at S of O as long as he did.

We tried to learn each other's ways. He was going to show me how to dance and I was going to teach him how to hunt and fish. Reuben loved to fish, but he had fished for carp and catfish in different kinds of waters than I had even seen, and he and his folks used cane poles. I had fished with cane poles with my grandparents on my mother's side, in my uncle's farm pond where we caught bass and bluegills. But I had been taught since I was young how to set trotlines and cast lures along the river for goggle-eye and smallmouth. Reuben didn't know what a Shakespeare casting reel was and I don't suppose he ever had seen a trotline.

I took him down to the School's big gravel bar on

Taneycomo to teach him how to fish for trout with cheese and he sat there the whole evening talking about his girlfriend. He didn't like the trout we cooked on hotplates in the dorm room. And my dance lesson was a fiasco. I told him that anyone who did that kind of thing exposed themselves to ridicule and I wasn't someone who could abide ridicule. I had never been to a dance in high school, never went to one in college and still haven't been to one today. Truthfully, I don't think everyone is born with rhythm. It was like my dad had often told me, "Everyone has something that they are born to be, born to do. But it is different with all men God created. You can't be what you ain't, so don't expect other folks to be what they ain't either."

Come Friday afternoon every couple of weeks, Reuben headed home, just as I did, but not for the same reasons. I was in love with the Big Piney River back home, and Reuben was in love with a girl. At the end of one semester I went into Reuben' dorm room and he was sitting there with big tears running down his face. He told me then that he was quitting school to go home and get married. His folks were really upset, because their son had a chance to get an education and opportunities better than they had ever had, and he was throwing it away to get married. I just told him I figured a man could get an education darn near anywhere if he was dedicated to doing that, and surely it wouldn't be any harder to go to school happy because he had a wife, than it would be going to school miserable because he didn't have. He brightened up just a little at that and I helped him carry down a suitcase or two. We shook hands and I never saw him again. I am sure his life turned out prosperous and happy.

I can't finish this without mentioning that a year or so later, at the University of Missouri I met the biggest, darkest man I have ever seen, living on the same floor as I. His name was Lynn Cox, and he was an offensive lineman for the MU football team. I walked into the dormitory restroom and there he was, standing there in his underwear brushing his teeth. He looked like a big brown mountain, really intimidating and scary. You have to remember I was about five-foot seven-inches tall and weighed less than 150 pounds. I took a big gulp and said hello. He broke into a big smile and we talked for about ten minutes or so.

Lynn was a little bit introverted, but a gentle person, and you could tell it immediately. I talked to him often, and got to know him well. I've got to tell you, I didn't meet more than a half dozen students at MU that I got to like really well, and Lynn was one of them. On that same floor was a future NFL wide receiver by the name of Mel Gray, and he and I talked a few times on elevators or in the hall. Mel was like Lynn, but not much bigger than me. You couldn't get him to say more than a few words in a quiet tone, and I never did get to know him.

On occasion, in that restroom, I would come across Lynn Cox and threaten to push him out of the way. A big smile would come across his face and he would make some comment about how I should be careful, because if he slipped and fell on me accidentally it might kill me.

One evening in the cafeteria I saw him sitting alone and I sat down to eat with him. He asked me if I was going to the football game on Saturday and I told him I had never yet been to one because I had to work on Saturdays either on campus or off, or at home. I lied about that. I was going home to go duck hunting with my dad. Lynn would never have understood that way of life I had.

And I couldn't understand his. He was quiet for a moment and he said, "You know what you tell me when I am around you? You tell me you don't hate me for the color of my skin!"

I was really taken aback. "Hate you?" I said, "I'm your friend. I admire you a great deal for who you are, not what you can do or where you come from or what color your skin is."

He didn't say anything, so I kept on, in a jestful tone… "I ought to hate you though," I said, "you are going to go play professional football and get rich and I am going to be lucky to get a job managing a pool hall. I'll probably be writing to you asking for a loan someday, so I have to stay on your good side."

Sure enough, Lynn played professional football and so did Mel Gray, who was a wide receiver of great renown for the St. Louis Cardinals.

It wasn't long after that that I was trying to get some sleep on Friday night in my dorm room, because I had to get up early and open the pool hall where I worked just off campus. It was getting late and there was some gosh-awful loud music coming from a room on another wing. The door was cracked just a little, so I pushed it open and there were about five or six dark-skinned students lounging around, some drinking and some smoking. They knew the R.A. on the floor, a wimpy guy by the name of Hawblitzler, wasn't going to say a word to them. So I did. "Fellows," I asked as nice as I could, "would you please turn down the music so some of us can sleep?"

You can guess what they called me… the favorite term of dark skinned hoodlums and gang members everywhere.

Those young men made it plain that they hated me, and in their little gang, they likely would have killed me if they could do it and get away with it. One of the athletes on that floor walked in behind me and spoke basically the same words and the music got turned down quickly.

I met plenty of those dark-skinned people at Missouri University that I really found to be despicable people. But now that I think of it, I know despicable people in the hills of the Ozarks too, no worse than they, no better… just of a different culture, a different way of life. Being worthless is something you find in all races. And it began to dawn on me that what would always separate light skinned and dark skinned people, was that difference in culture. There was a difference in what we wanted in our lives. There was a difference in our backgrounds, in our goals, our beliefs, and our traditions. There is a difference in what we are as human beings!

I absolutely love to hear the dark-skinned choirs and the old songs they refer to even today as 'negro spirituals'. But I can't say that I would feel at home in one of their churches, because those country churches I went to, and the churches Reuben went to were as different as night and day. And yet we were there to worship the same Son of God.

Out of college, I took a job as Chief Naturalist for the Arkansas State Park System, and for a time I had a little office in the basement of the state capitol building. I got to know two young dark-skinned men who worked there, and I liked them both. I took note that the two of them were as different from each other as I was from each of them. But I became close friends with one. His name was William Davis, but he made it known that he was known as Willie and that's what he wanted to be called.

On those days when I worked in that office and wasn't traveling, Willie and I went out on a back section of the capitol lawn and played wiffle ball during the lunch hour. I would give a fortune to have films and tapes of those games. I liked Willie very much. He was bright and vociferous and a natural born comedian. Sometimes I couldn't play ball for laughing. But we had some great wiffle ball games.

I had a baby girl at home and Willie had a baby at home too. One day I told him that I would like for his wife to meet my wife and if he could pick a time I would bring my family to his home to meet his. Willie became very serious, when he told me that could never happen. I didn't understand.

"Where I live," he said, "you don't want to go, and I don't want the people around me knowing I have a friend like you… they wouldn't approve of that."

I lived out in the woods in the north part of the county in a little home far from suburbs and closed in neighborhoods, maybe thirty miles from where my office was located. Willie lived in east Little Rock, in a community where white people didn't go and weren't really welcome.

And that's when I realized that we live in a society of racists, and it will likely be that way forever because racism is taught to new generations over and over. But racism is a two-way thing. Many dark-skinned people feel hatred for whites for no other reason than skin color. It has been taught to them, and bad experiences with just a few light skinned people reinforce it. They cannot realize that there are so many of us who harbor no resentment or hatred toward them. They are racist and no one can deny it!

And then there are those of my race who feel hatred of dark-skinned people because they have seen too many newscasts on television where they show people rioting in cities, and gangs of young men with caps cocked sideways and their pants down around their butts, giving the impression that they and all of their color and age are criminals.

I can say this... I would hate to be anywhere near those dark-skinned people I see in Chicago and Detroit and Los Angeles, but I would have been proud to have Willie Davis, Lynn Cox and Reuben as neighbors. I would have had no fear of my little girls growing up and playing with the children of those men.

But I know that in America those who can live like that in respect and peace are always going to be the exception rather than the rule. Racism is a two way street, and hatred is hatred, existing in men of all colors and all nationalities. Willie tried to tell me that, while assuring me that we could be great friends without changing our cultures. And I grew to understand it as I grew older. I saw hatred in one race that was just as strong as any you could find in another.

I came to realize that the way things were, people in the United States wanted to be equal but separate. We HAD to be equal but separate. And that didn't come from a light skinned country boy like me, it came from a dark skinned young man who lived in a city suburb.

Those of the two different races have to realize someday that we do not hate each other as much as we fear each other. The big ingredient in racism is fear, even more than hatred. To tell you the truth, I am afraid of the dark skinned culture I see on television. Lynn Cox looked at me, half his size and he was afraid that I was thinking badly of him, finding fault with him because of color.

My dad pointed out to me that God instructs men to love not just those who are easy to love, but those who are hard to love as well. You have to get old to understand that, I believe. But meeting Reuben there at School of the Ozarks made me learn at a young age that while God made us different, He made us capable of feeling respect, concern, and caring for each other despite those differences. I do not go out of my way to become different than I am created to be, but I understand that on occasion when men of two colors have to mingle together there should be a willingness to help each other as best we can, to think of the other person and make sacrifices for others before we think of ourselves. I think that's what Jesus meant when he spoke of each of us learning to love our fellow man.

I didn't understand that when I was just a kid at School of the Ozarks, but it is the place where I began to learn it. I am glad that the first dark skinned person I ever met was a kid a lot like me, but different.

I will make my opinions about a man based on who he is and what he does, not on his color. So maybe it is time we started classing people differently than 'black' and 'white'. Lets say it like it is. We are black, brown, tan, beige, ochre, golden and cream-colored. Then let's separate people according to who is bad and good, and maybe several steps in between the two. And when that is done, in the long run, color won't have a thing to do with who falls into any of those good to bad categories.

When it is all said and done, we will never see an end to racism on this earth, but it will dwindle away little by little. Most of us won't have any part of it. This nation's news media will ignore us to concentrate on the strife and hatred.

Looking back at things as a grown man, watching all the problems between two races, I want to stay away from either of those sides. As I said, if I had Lynn or Willie or Reuben as neighbors, that would be fine with me, but they'd be disappointed living out here in the woods of the rural Ozarks. I have seen nor heard nothing of any of them since my early twenties. But I never called them anything but friends of mine.

Chapter 25

FINDING FAITH

The chaplain at S of O was Reverend Schimpf. A strange name for a preacher... back home preachers had simpler names, Morton, Baker, Jones, those kinds of names. Mr. Schimpf had two daughters, one in the S of O high school, and one a freshman in college. I never talked to either of them the whole time I was there, but they were both very pretty and they got a great deal of attention from college boys. It came to me, as I was thinking about it one day, that it would be a great deal easier for a preacher to have homely daughters. Reverend Schimpf was a very devout, good man, but I don't suppose I ever talked with him either. I listened to his sermons on those Sundays when we had to be in the chapel for church service and he made good sense. As much as I would have liked to skip chapel service to go fishing on Taneycomo, I have to admit that I was better off because I went, heard what he said and thought about it. I hadn't done that much before because I sat on the back row in church when I was younger and dozed off a lot. Even today, I find it very hard to stay awake in church.

Being forced to go to church on Sunday likely is not

the best way to get close to God. But as I recall Dad and Mom had forced me to go to church for years. Had they not, I would have been outdoors on each Sunday morning hunting or fishing or exploring. When I was thirteen years old I was half asleep one Sunday night when our preacher, who was very limited in education and not the smartest man you'd ever meet, tricked several of us kids into coming up to the altar.

Now I am not saying he wasn't a dedicated and enthusiastic Christian because he was. My dad told me that our preacher and his wife once were real rounders, found in one of the local taverns or dance halls every Saturday night when they were young. Somehow they both repented and turned into the Lord's servants, and I can tell you, it wasn't phony... they believed. The two of them had been on both sides of the road and they were bent on seeing to it that no one else made the mistakes they had. Trouble was, old Ervin only knew one sermon and he preached every way he could. Hellfire waited for those who didn't get converted as he thought was best.

I knelt at that altar that night thinking I was up there to help pray for somebody and the next thing I knew he was kneeling down beside me with tears in his eyes asking me if I wanted to be saved. I said it was okay with me and then he started telling me what to say and I said it. I went home that night thinking that I might ought to check my pocket to see if I still had the quarter I started out with. The preacher, I do believe, thought his value in the eyes of God depended on how many souls he brought to that altar, by whatever means and methods necessary.

I had to be baptized in the Big Piney in March, and I kept wondering why we couldn't put it off until July. I nearly froze, and I had no idea what it was all about. My gosh, I had only been thirteen years old for a few months! I was relieved somewhat because the preacher said I was assured of not going to hell. Our preacher had me convinced he knew who was going to heaven and who wasn't, and he told me I was safe, for sure. I got to praying a lot after that, and one of my regular prayers was that God would find a way to snuff out one particular school bully that I couldn't see any value in whatsoever. Many, many years later I found out that the kid I wanted to see killed by an avenging angel had turned his life around. I had no idea that God might actually spare some no account like him knowing that someday he would be different, almost like he was reborn!

But I will say one thing about that little Free-Will Baptist church where I was forced to go… there were several men there who were friends of my dad who never told me what Christians should be, they showed me. My dad, who was the greatest man I ever knew, said he knew that old Ervin, the preacher, wasn't Billy Graham, but he said going to church would give me some things I needed when I grew older, and when those times came, I would remember that he wasn't threatening me within an inch of my life if I didn't go to church, for no reason.

So here I was at School of the Ozarks, seventeen years old, still going to church because I had to. And once again, I was hoping that sometime Mark McWorthless and his friends would get drunk and fall off the overlook at the west end of the college and be found the next day drowned in Taneycomo Lake.

But I was beginning to understand things just a little. Some folks went into that chapel and heard Christ speaking to them, and felt the presence of God because He made them different than He had made me. I didn't feel anything there and my thoughts drifted to some test coming up, or one of the girls in Memorial Hall. I felt God's presence when I was over on the lake at Clevenger Cove or on the Big Piney camping on a gravel bar when the sun dipped into another realm and began a new day somewhere else. I talked to God in a more serious manner, wanting him to tell me He was real and helping me to understand and learn about what the difference was between what Jesus wanted of a man, and what God wanted. I was confused.

And then there were those Bible study nights in the dormitory, when Christian boys and non-believers got together and argued, with everyone trying to talk at once and seeing who could be the loudest. Each side had good arguments, with Mark McWorthless wanting to know if God could create a rock so big He couldn't lift it?

I learned something about futility at some of those two or three hour contests between the Scribes and the Pharisees and the School of the Ozarks apostles. I remember that one boy who was the son of a minister back in his hometown, was one of the strongest Christians there at first, but in a few months he got dissuaded, I guess, and fell in with some guys who took off on Saturday nights to drink booze and chase women in Springfield, Branson or Rockaway Beach. But I figure when he grew older and got his fill of that, he went back to the basis of his beliefs and teachings and got straightened out.

And I guess, though it pains me to say it, that I am hoping Mark McWorthless and some of those really evil kids at S of O got over being evil and turned toward their maker to become what He wanted them to be. That seems to happen a lot, when someone who is worthless when they are young grows into manhood, gets married and raises children and in time begins to get old and somehow becomes worth something after all.

As for me, I never had the slightest idea what God wanted of me, never knew what faith was all about until I was about twenty-five years old, and I spent a cold, bright Sunday morning alone out on Bull Shoals Lake watching the snow spitting down here and there. My wife and two little daughters were in church, and I had gone to Bull Shoals to get some driftwood for a wood carver in Illinois who said he would give me five hundred dollars for a pick-up load. I will say more about that driftwood in chapter 21 and the importance it played in my life, because it goes back to the two years I spent at School of the Ozarks with Table Rock so close at hand.

With a wife and two little girls, I began to realize that as a writer, I wasn't a great provider. Even with my weekly newspaper columns and work as a naturalist in the Arkansas mountains during those early years, some of the magazine articles I wrote and sold took a long time to get paid for, and bills would come due which needed immediate attention. That driftwood on Bull Shoals helped me to make ends meet, but with that and the writing and the work I was doing for the Arkansas Natural Heritage Commission, I was putting in some 70 and 80-hour weeks working at what I loved to do.

It didn't leave any time for church and besides that I didn't want to be there. That made me feel like I was an outcast. That morning, watching them walk up the sidewalk to the First Baptist Church in Harrison, Arkansas all dressed up and so beautiful, as I drove past in my old pick-up, dressed in old ragged coveralls and work boots, I felt awful. I was as confused and as low as a man can get, knowing that in the church where my little girls and my wife were, I was as out of place as a coonhound at the Vatican. I was thinking that if I had good life insurance my family would be better off if I drowned in the lake, but I was a long way from suicidal.

So out on the Lake, I sat down on a log and talked to God. That is the day He revealed to me a little about who I was and what He expected of me and what a belief in Jesus was all about. All that is of no importance to those good people who actually WERE Christians who were in church that morning, it was just between Him and me. I heard the voice of God, not in a voice someone else could have heard, but in a voice only I could have heard, and it was real. I was told strong and sure… "You are what I made you, and that is good. Do not try to be someone else whom I have made different than you. Don't be ashamed of who you are, and do not be overly proud, just be who you are, all the time, with all people. Spend your life thinking more of others than yourself."

That morning, I felt as if my feet were not touching the ground as I worked, and I found beautiful driftwood everywhere, enough to fill that pickup of mine in only a few hours. I felt a contentedness and happiness that morning that so many proclaim from a trip to the altar that makes them born again.

Somehow I think that the basis for that wonderful morning alone with God on Bull Shoals was from the base I began to build at School of the Ozarks. I got a little closer to that understanding not so much from what I was told while I was there, but from what I was shown with the lives of some of the most wonderful people I have ever known, named in these chapters.

There are miracles in the lives of everyone if they recognize them. I have never heard the voice of God from a burning bush, but we have talked often when I am out in the woods or on the river. The prayers I sent forth when I was young asked for much…the health of my family, help in paying the bills, a relief from the back pain which once tormented me. And I often asked for the guidance I needed when decisions had to be made. And yes, I have had to ask for forgiveness…an awful lot. Now as I grow older, my prayers are more and more, honest utterances of thanks. Nothing fancy, nothing said in the presence of others… just a genuine, sincere praise in this un-flowery hillbilly dialect of mine.

At the end of my life I want it to be said of me that no matter how poorly I have done in my life, there was no doubt ever that I knew how simple Christianity really was…. just putting others before myself. And I want everyone to say that there was no doubt in Larry Dablemont's faith in Jesus, the Son of God. And if I have enough money for a headstone when that time comes, I want it to be noted that I spent some of my youth on the Big Piney River, in a pool hall at Houston, Mo., and at a place called School of the Ozarks.

Chapter 26

CHARLENE & GLORIA JEAN

There were some fine teachers at School of the Ozarks, many older instructors who had worked at universities around the country in younger years. Dr. Poole and Dr. Stone were two who were most likely in their early seventies. I never did figure out what Dr. Poole taught, never did attend a class he taught. But he was a close friend of Dr. Alice Allen Nightingale, and because of that, after working at her home on weekends for extra money, I ended up working for Dr. Poole in a very extravagant flower garden he had in his back yard. It had exotic plants and sculptures and pools and fountains, and it was beautiful. Over my two years at S of O, I made much of my spending money working after school hours for him, earning about a dollar and a quarter an hour. I know Dr. Poole hoped someday when he was gone his garden would be continued and preserved, and I don't know if that happened. I think his home still is in use but the garden behind it is likely gone. He was a very effeminate person with a full head of white hair and a white mustache. He just shuffled along, and directed my work on his gardens with a difficulty in walking over the rough ground.

My friend Dane Allen and I built a nice storage shed for him right behind his home, maybe an eight by ten building where he could keep a mower and tools. Some time after it was built, and only a couple of weeks before I left S of O to attend the University of Missouri, I met a beautiful young lady by the name of Charlene, whom I may have become very serious about if I had had more time. One Sunday evening that summer I took her to Dr. Poole's garden and showed her all I had done, traveling the circular path I had created. Dr. Poole was gone on a vacation, and when I showed her the little tool shed that Dane and I had built, I closed the door behind us. I put my arms around her and held her close and told her that in all my life I had never met a girl like her, saying all the things that 18-year-old boys say while trying their best to sound serious.

I pulled her close and kissed her a couple of times, and she looked into my eyes and said, "If we got caught in here like this, they would throw us both out of school!" I told her I knew that, then leaned closer for another kiss. But she pushed me back just a little, and continued. "Wouldn't it be awful to be thrown out of school for doing nothing more than kissing me in someone's tool shed?"

I got the message, it was her way of telling me that our date was going nowhere beyond a few kisses, and we could do that in front of the dormitory like everyone else did. We left the storage shed to walk through the garden and around campus, holding hands. I had no boundaries as to what that date would lead to, being young and stupid and incapable of thinking more than fifteen minutes ahead, but Charlene did. We went to the chapel service that evening and I saw that she took her faith very seriously. At that time I didn't. I just went to chapel service because it was a required thing.

We sat in that big beautiful chapel after the service was over and I asked her if she would like to wear my high school ring until I left school in about three weeks. She said she would, and she put it on and wore it the whole time I knew her. I decided I wanted her to keep it after I left, but Charlene said no. She knew somehow that we didn't know each other well enough to think we would ever see each other again. I have no idea why I took it back, because she was about everything I had dreamed of. She had long shining black hair and a big smile that never left her face. She was thin and shapely, and happy and intelligent, and I had a sense that whoever married her someday was going to be an awful lucky guy. But I have to admit I thought about marrying every girl I had more than two dates with, going back to that little 14-year-old girl from our church in Houston. I had never ever had a really good friend who was a girl. That's what Charlene was for me… a really good female friend. It really wasn't a romance, but a friendship.

Charlene

For some reason, I had never considered a life past the age of twenty-one without a wife and family. For most of us young men only 18 or 19 years old, such thinking is dangerous, because we consider ourselves men, not knowing how much we will change in a few years, and how poor we are when we are young at judging a girl's character and personality. For most of us who get married before we are 25, it is sort of the luck of the draw. I knew a pair of kids there at S of O who had been going together since high school, and they were constantly together and in love for four years there at School of the Ozarks. They were married upon graduation and were divorced a year later. How in the world can that happen?

When I got to the University of Missouri, I didn't meet many girls I had a thing in common with. But for some reason, Charlene and I never wrote letters back and forth or communicated at all. That first year at MU was rough. I didn't like it then and I never did, even though I met some wonderful people and two lifelong friends. I missed S of O and the kind of people that were there. At MU I was a number--133746. In many of the classes the professor never showed up, you heard lectures from his student assistants who were working on Master's degrees, and they were all liberal as hell. When you took a test, you didn't get the paper back, you just looked at a big list on the door where your grade was posted by your number. My number, 133746, usually got a C, and I was happy to get it. In many of those classes, the textbooks were too expensive for me, and I did without. A friend I met back then, Dennis Whiteside, who loved to hunt and fish and became one of those close life-long friends, often let me use one of his books when I had to study for a test. Today if he asks to borrow anything from me, he mentioned how he once loaned me books and we still laugh a lot about those old times.

But it was a lonely time as well. I didn't meet many girls I wanted to date, and I didn't have enough money to take them places. I had my old '56 Chevy and it sat parked during the week, without much gas in it. But, the girls at MU just weren't like Charlene. And while there had to some poor kids there, you never saw them. The kids were either very well off or smart enough to win scholarships out of high school. Those are two categories I didn't fall into.

Today when people ask me where I got my wildlife management degree, I tell them, but I always add that the better half of it came from School of the Ozarks. A year or so back, the University of Missouri decided to start honoring Wiccan and voodoo holidays, honoring those students of the occult. They have decided that to pay proper respect to diversity I suppose… because at MU there was just about everything on campus you could imagine. If you wanted to act like you were some addle brained high school kid, you could join a fraternity. But I spent most of my two and one-half years there either going to class or working. I got a campus job, fifteen hours a week, at the Archaeology Department, and then found a nice little pool hall just off the east side of campus, and I worked there at night, usually about twenty hours a week. It turned out to be a lot like it was at S of O, except you had to work a lot more hours to pay for everything. I still went back home in the spring and fall and worked on the Big Piney guiding hunters and fishermen a little, and trapping some in the during the winter holiday break. Everything I did was about making money and paying what University of

Missouri wanted of me.

When I finished my first year at MU, enrolled as a wildlife management major in the school of Agriculture, I learned that the state park system was hiring summer naturalists to work in the state parks, and I submitted my application. I was called in for an interview and hired on the spot. I knew little about the state parks of Missouri, and with my background on the Big Piney River I should have chosen a park on a river like Montauk or Roaring River, but I noted that Table Rock State Park on Table Rock Lake was only a few miles from School of the Ozarks! What a break for a kid who missed those folks as much as I did. In late May I drove down to the park with two sets of new uniforms, and immediately went to the campus to see Dr. Nightingale and Dr. Clark and Charlene. But she wasn't there. Charlene had met another young man shortly after I left, and had quit school to get married. I never saw her again.

I learned that about ten years later that Charlene, happily married with two children, had been driving to work just outside of Branson when she was hit head-on by a driver swerving into her lane and was killed instantly. I could have cried when I heard that. I wish I could someday meet her children and tell them I was a friend of their mother and what a wonderful person she was.

At Table Rock State Park that summer I built trails and took people on hikes and gave night programs. I learned that it was something I was made for. I had grown up in the outdoors, and I knew all about trees and birds and fish and mammals, the subjects I was studying in classes at Missouri University. It was easy to teach and interpret nature for others, most of them city people who loved to go on hikes and attend my evening programs, which regularly pulled in 200 campers for an audience.

I gained a tremendous confidence I had never had, even as I matured at School of the Ozarks. I knew I had found my niche in life. In years to come I would work for a time as Chief Naturalist for Arkansas State Parks and then for awhile as a Naturalist at Buffalo River for the National Park Service as I built my credentials as an outdoor writer. But that summer at Table Rock gave me the confidence that I could do anything. For the first time I felt that I was anyone's equal, despite the fact I didn't have much money. When a kid who felt as insignificant as I had felt in high school turns around that abruptly, it is something of a miracle, and there hadn't been many miracles to that point in my life unless I count winning a snooker tournament or catching that 35-pound flathead catfish out of the Big Piney. But I think what was about to happen, has to be referred to as a genuine miracle.

Sometime late in the summer, a Government Auditing Office accountant from Florissant, Mo., a suburb of St. Louis, took his family on their regular summer vacation, where they would camp at Lake of the Ozarks for two weeks as they had for years. It would be hard to convince me today that God wasn't watching, doing a great deal more planning than I had ever been known for. Frank Goedde and his wife and three kids all missed the Lake of the Ozarks State Park turnoff where they had been going for ten years or more, and traveled all the way down Interstate 44 until that exit was just was too far back to turn around. That's when Mr. Goedde made a decision he may have regretted for years. He decided to go on down to Table Rock State Park to camp, a place his family had never vacationed before, where I was waiting.

Working and living with a couple of guys who were about my age, we had developed a competition, trying to see who could date the most girls from other states. I had already had a date with a girl from Mississippi and another from Oklahoma and one from Illinois, but I was way behind Ron Housman and Terry Shipman. The two of them worked on park crews, dumping garbage and cleaning restrooms and mowing. I had an edge in that I walked through campgrounds talking to campers each day, telling them about the evening programs and hikes they could go on with me. But I still was well behind in the contest, because Ron and Terry had really nice cars and were quite a bit better looking than me. Those are two things which make quite a handicap when you are trying to impress the girls.

I had to use my brain. So I went to the gate attendant and asked him to let me know every time some teen-aged girl from out of state came through with her family that was reasonably good looking, at least a four on a scale of one to ten. When Frank Goedde drove through that night in July, the attendant saw something in the darkness in the rear window of his car about Florida. Turned out, it was a window sticker which read, "Florissant Valley Community College", where Mr. Goedde's daughter Gloria Jean, was a first-year student. The gate attendant also noted that she was asleep in the back seat, and was fairly attractive, as best he could see. He said he thought she might be an eight or nine on that scale we had. Heck, when I saw her, I thought she was a twelve! Then he told me the campsite number and I knew there was no way Ron or Terry could beat me there.

I went by their campsite that next morning while they

were fixing breakfast. Their younger daughter and son were up, but the older girl was still in the tent, and I didn't get to see her. I lingered awhile and told the younger kids all about this fantastic hike I was about to embark on at 10 a.m. where they could see the Ozarks at its most natural, maybe even a deer or a bear or whatever.

The little girl and her older brother came, and their folks made their big sister go along to watch over them. That didn't make her real happy, the way I understand it. The first time I saw Gloria Jean Goedde she was there at the laundromat-meeting place with about twenty hikers, wearing clean white tennis shoes and white shorts and an orange and brown blouse with a silly looking floppy-brimmed pink hat.

It was love at first sight. For me... not her! She had the look of someone who wanted to be sleeping late. She stood there with her arms folded, looking off into the distance, bouncing her knee up and down wanting to get the whole thing over with, clearly exasperated. She fell in at the end of the line well behind her siblings and off into the woods we went.

Gloria Jean did love the outdoors, and nature. Right off, you could see that she was impressed with what I knew, and she started kind of enjoying herself. I learned later that when her little sister started telling her parents what a smart, good-looking naturalist I was, Gloria told them I was only about 15 or 16 years old! What the heck, I didn't care if she wasn't interested in me. She was way too pretty and stuck up for me and she wasn't from Florida, so she wasn't going to help me win the contest with Ron and Terry.

You have to remember that most campers didn't stay long at the state park. If you took out a girl from Oklahoma you tallied up one point for a new state and she was gone a day or so later and you tried to find one from Kansas or Iowa. But the Goedde family intended to stay there for two weeks and their daughter wouldn't even get me one point!

After the hike that morning, I handed out pamphlets from the Conservation Department about snakes. I had car trunk full of them, but when I got to Gloria Jean's little sister and brother, I had somehow run out of them. See what I mean about using my brains. That took some doing! I told them that I had several kinds of nature pamphlets up at my office in the park headquarters, and if they would go with me I would get them several. Gloria Jean shook her head 'no' at first, but I talked her into it. I took them to the office and gave them pamphlets on snakes and birds and plants and everything else I could find, and then took them back to their campsite where I got to meet their parents, who seemed like great people. I probably ought to inject here that few men ever meet their future mother-in-law and figure right off what kind of problem she is going to be for them years down the line.

But meeting my future mother-in-law that day was the farthest thing from my mind.

Chapter 27

YEARS THAT PASSED TOO FAST

I kept thinking about the young lady, realizing that since she wasn't actually from Florida I ought to forget her. But it was hard not to think about her. I set out during my lunch hour to ask her for a date, but I had to find her and she hadn't meant to be found. I had to get her little sister's help.

Gloria Jean Goedde and me at Table Rock State Park in 1968, a few days after our first date, a visit to School of the Ozarks College.

She told me that Gloria Jean was hiding out down on a big rock below their camp, in her swimsuit and hair curlers, taking in some sun and reading a book. So I went looking for her. Was she ever surprised to see me!!!

Even in those curlers, she was gorgeous. I asked her if I could take her out that evening to see the most wonderful place in Southern Missouri, the School of the Ozarks. She said no. Thirty minutes later she told me that she would go with me if I would just leave and let her finish the book.

I took her to Dr. Poole's garden right off, claiming credit for the wonder and beauty of it, and showing her the little storage shed that Dane and I had built. She wouldn't go near it. We spent the whole evening at School of the Ozarks, where Gloria Jean learned I wasn't a young kid after all, and marveled at the place where I had pursued an education for two years, working my way through. I think she was really impressed when I took her to meet the college president, and Dr. Clark was happy to see me. He even bragged on me a little. I found out that Gloria Jean knew a president too. She was attending college and working part-time at the office of a vice president of McDonnell Douglas Aircraft. And she could type 105 words a minute!!!!

It was a great evening, and I learned how quiet and shy she was. She had spent her school days going to a Catholic girls' school, where she wore a uniform all through grade school and three years of high school. That night I didn't pay much attention to what she said, but I was enthralled with the fact she could type 105 words per minute without error! For an aspiring writer who could only type about 35 words per minute with six or eight errors, things were beginning to fall together. And for someone as outgoing and gregarious as me, it was wonderful to meet a beautiful girl who listened while I talked, and didn't say a whole lot.

I had the disadvantage of driving an old '56 Chevy while Ron and Terry both had sleek, newer model cars. Ron drove a burgundy Pontiac GTO and Terry Shipman had a black Chevy Supersport if I remember, both about eight or nine years younger than my old car. Ron stopped by their camp and met the family, and talked to Gloria Jean and her folks. That night back at our cabin, he very seriously talked with me about how young men our age needed to enjoy our lives and not get too carried away with any girl. He ended it by telling me…"That girl in Camp 38, from Florissant… she is the marrying kind! You need to be careful. " "With her," he said, "you could wind up married."

Didn't I wish for something like that? But it wasn't likely, I wasn't quite the scoundrel Ron and Terry were, but the older I got, the more they were rubbing off on me.

For the next couple of evenings, the Goedde family came to my evening programs and I always talked Gloria Jean into letting me walk her back to camp. She would be gone during the day with her family, to places they wanted to see. I think she took them all to School of the Ozarks one day, something that really impressed her dad. He had to have gotten the idea I was made of something special to be accepted to a college like that.

The first chance I got, I asked Gloria Jean for another date. I was afraid if I didn't take her out and spend some money on her, she would get to thinking I was a deadbeat with an old car, and start looking at Ron Houseman as a better prospect. This time, she said yes without me having to stand around and beg. I was making progress. I took her to the fish hatchery down below Table Rock Dam and spent a quarter buying fish food, and then we went to the little restaurant across from the park, where the owner, Joe Standlee, caused Gloria Jean to see red flags.

He brought us our hamburgers and French fries and looked at Gloria Jean for a moment and back at me.... "Is this another sister? Boy, you got more sisters than anyone I have ever met!"

I tried to explain the remark to her after he had left. My sister Muriel was a freshman at S of O. I will talk more about her in another chapter, but she and about three or four of her roommates came to the park one weekend early in the summer in an old car with bedrolls and a tent to go camping. I had saved them a site and paid for it, and they were really enjoying themselves until Saturday night about midnight when a couple of drunk high school boys found out about them and kept driving around trying to get the girls to go swimming with them. Muriel came up to the cabin where I was sleeping with the whole carful of girls, scared to death they were being harassed by a carload of wild-eyed killers. So I drove down and parked my car at their campsite and when the boys came around, I told them that if I saw them again I would contact a park ranger and have them taken to jail. They vamoosed, and I slept the rest of the night in my car, wishing that those girls had come camping without my sister.

The next morning I took them all to breakfast and had Joe Standlee put it on my credit sheet. I told him that Muriel was my sister. He looked at all the girls and asked if they were all my sisters. I just told him they were, and they all laughed, as Joe did.

I realized that Gloria Jean and I were making some headway against her shy and suspicious nature when she actually believed me. But just to be sure, she wanted to meet

Muriel. My younger sister, who was the 4.0 valedictorian at Houston High School, and soon to be the 4.0 valedictorian at School of the Ozarks, always made me look good. It was easy to see that Gloria Jean, after meeting my sister, thought I might have a lot more going for me than it appeared. It would be years before she knew that a 2.5 grade point was the highest semester average I had ever mustered.

Today as a writer and naturalist, I speak often to church groups, wild game dinners, school groups etc. I tell them a little about meeting Gloria Jean, and while it doesn't have much truth to it, I tell a story that breaks everyone up about the night I took Gloria Jean to a drive-in movie in Branson, just before her family went back home. She tolerates it, knowing that if it is the biggest lie I ever tell, it will surprise everyone. I tell about how I put a wood console in the front seat of my old '56 Chevy, and while at the drive-in that night I found that because of it I couldn't get as close to her as I would like, and how I couldn't even really get my arm around her.

I interject here that as a kid in the pool hall, I had often been told by the Front Bench Regulars, the old men who came in to watch snooker games and tell longwinded stories, to remember two things when I came to a point where I was considering marriage. They all agreed that it is best to marry the prettiest girl you ever met and try to find one that isn't real smart, so she won't figure out just what you are up to half the time.

So there we were at the drive in, watching John Wayne put out oil fires in some movie I didn't want to watch anyway, since it wasn't a western. I got over as close to Gloria Jean as I could and while she was eating a bag of popcorn, I whispered low, "Honey, would you like to get in the back seat."

She looked at me and whispered back... "No, I want to stay up here with you!"

Right then, I remembered the advice those old men gave me, and I realized that while she was the prettiest girl I had ever seen, she certainly wasn't the smartest.

Gloria Jean's folks came back for a weekend just before I went back to MU and I took her up on the high peak looking out over Table Rock Lake they called Baird Mountain, where I proposed she take my high school ring back home with her. That night, I think I knew I would never see that ring again unless I bought her another one.

That fall, when I wasn't going home to hunt and fish, I was driving over to Florissant to see Gloria Jean, and finally I got to where I would go get her and take her with me to Houston for a weekend, where she got to meet my folks. My elderly grandmother, Hilda McNew, just loved her. My grandmother had prayed for me since I was a little boy, and you cannot convince me that her prayers went unheeded. It had to be her prayers that got me into college at S of O, if you consider the miracle of a kid occupying fifth place on an admission office waiting list, and being the last freshman accepted after five other students dropped out the first week. She told me that there was no doubt that Gloria Jean was the one for me... as if I didn't already know that. And very seriously she told Gloria that she loved her, even if she was a Catholic.

My grandmother passed away back in Houston one afternoon in early October, and that weekend Gloria took a bus down to Rolla, where I met her and took her home with me. Grandma McNew's funeral was on a Saturday afternoon, so while Gloria ate breakfast with my sisters and parents, I went into Houston to see my old friend Ned Casebeer, who owned a jewelry shop right next to our pool hall. I told him I would bring Gloria Jean in after the funeral, just before closing time. I told him I needed some time to pay for her engagement ring, and he told me he would give me all year with no interest. But then I had a strange request. I asked him if he would take out all the rings that he could sell me for 300 dollars, so I could have her pick which one she wanted without putting me in debt until I was an old man. Ned complied. He lined up all the rings across the counter top which cost from 300 to 400 dollars and told me I could have whichever one she picked for 300 dollars, with 50 dollars down and payments of 25 dollars a month until the ring was paid off.

After the funeral, I took Gloria for a walk down Main Street to see the old pool hall where I had worked as a boy, only four years before. I had never formally proposed, though I think I had already told her that if I ever was crazy enough to think about getting married, I would probably ask her first and give her the right of first refusal. When I steered her into that jewelry shop, where Ned Casebeer was waiting with a grin on his face like a possum in a persimmon tree, Gloria had a couple of dozen rings to choose from, and she figured out that for once, I was serious. That week ahead of us, Gloria Jean turned 19 and I turned 20. She never dreamed that when she turned 19 she would be wearing an engagement ring. It all seemed so right to me. Our first date had been at School of the Ozarks, just as I always figured it would be. And the preacher who was going to marry us was Dr. M. Graham Clark.

We set the wedding date for the following June, and to her mother's chagrin, Gloria left the Catholic Church to join me in going to little churches at which denominations meant little. It didn't seem to bother her dad as much. Maybe it was because he was a Lutheran. She picked out a beautiful big Presbyterian church for her wedding, and we changed our wedding date from June to the last weekend of March. That abrupt change caused many of her relatives, and mine I suppose, to jump to conclusions. They didn't know that we changed the date because it was the beginning of spring break, which afforded us a weeklong honeymoon, and we had to work the wedding around Dr. Clark's schedule.

On May 29th my old friend and boss, the president of School of the Ozarks College who was also an ordained Presbyterian minister, flew to St. Louis from New Orleans, Louisiana with his wife Elizabeth, where he had been appearing at an event raising funds for the college.

The church was packed, and six of my friends showed up to be groomsmen, since Gloria Jean wanted six bridesmaids in her wedding. I am telling you, it is a job to get six of my friends, all single, to skip the first weekend of spring break to go to a wedding, especially when all six of them were sure the whole wedding was a mistake.

Dr. Clark got to the church about fifteen minutes before the 11:00 a.m. wedding, and he calmed me down a lot and told me what to expect and how to get through it. Knowing I didn't have much money, I think Gloria Jean's dad tried to pay him something, but Dr. Clark wouldn't hear of it. He said it was an honor for him and Elizabeth to be asked to be a part of my wedding. He never could know what an honor it was for me to have him there.

When the wedding was over, he asked me if I would consider bringing my new bride to the guesthouse at School

of the Ozarks, the beautiful house overlooking Lake Taneycomo, where some of the best-known guests of the school had stayed. On our honeymoon, we took a trip down to Harrison, Arkansas and Eureka Springs and some places we had both wanted to see. We returned that night to the campus and the guesthouse, and for the next two days we fished for trout on Taneycomo. Most of the time I spent baiting hooks for Gloria Jean and netting her fish. One day she caught her limit and mine too. On the last afternoon we fished there, I used a top-of-the-line Ambassadeur reel she had bought me as a wedding present and caught a 5- or 6-pound rainbow trout. Gloria Jean suggested it might be my best catch ever, but I assured her she was. Looking up at the bluff above us where you could see the library and the Nettie Marie Jones Learning Center and the spire of the Chapel high in the air, I realized how much God had blessed me. I was still a year away from getting my degree at MU, but what could stop me now?

I did indeed graduate from M.U. in January of 1970 with a degree in wildlife management. We went to Arkansas where we bought a little home out in the country and I worked for a year as the Outdoor Editor of the state's largest daily newspaper, The Arkansas Democrat. It was amazing how things happened. In one year, the Chief Naturalist job was created at the Arkansas State Park system, and I got that job. But at the Democrat, they allowed me to continue writing my outdoor column, which I kept writing for ten or twelve years.

I don't believe I have lived one month of my life without writing a regular outdoor column for some newspaper somewhere. Today my self-syndicated outdoor column goes to about 30 newspapers in three states. I wrote my first magazine article for Outdoor Life in 1971 and since that time I have written about 700 magazine articles for fifteen or twenty different outdoor magazines. I published my first book in 1985 and have written 8 more since then. I started my own Publishing Company in 1999.

Most of our lives, while our three daughters were growing up, we lived on a wooded ridgetop west of Harrison, Arkansas where I did some contract work for the state's Natural Heritage Commission, studying and reporting on natural areas in the Ozark and Ouachita mountains.

In 1990, we moved to our present home about ten miles from Bolivar, Mo. when my two oldest daughters started to college up here, one in Springfield and one in Bolivar. My oldest daughter, Lori, got her medical degree at Missouri University and is a doctor today, and her younger sister Christy attended Southwest Baptist University and today teaches high school science classes. Like her dad, Christy worked for many years as a State Park Naturalist in the summer.

Gloria and I still go visit S of O from time to time. About 28 years after our honeymoon at the guesthouse, we took our youngest daughter, Leah, to S of O where she moved into the same dorm room I had moved into when I was only 17 years old. She would graduate and become a computer software expert with a company called Wide Orbit. I am very fortunate to have all three of my girls living within just a few miles of us. For that, I thank God on a regular basis.

When we left Leah there at School of the Ozarks, it was a very emotional moment for me. It seemed like only yesterday… Now the last of my little girls was all grown up and on her own. I started to give her some advice, and then I thought back to the time when I got there as just a kid with so much to learn, and I decided against it.

The School got me off to a good start, and took care of me, and shaped me into what I would become. It would do the same for her!

In 2001, my youngest daughter, Leah, graduated from School of the Ozarks, by then renamed College of the Ozarks. I envy her... I wish I had.

Cover painting by Duane Hada, Mountain Home, Arkansas

THANKS...

I want to thank S of O students Christian Gray, Paytience Markle and Amberly Anderson for helping me get many of the old photos found here. I'd also like to thank student Dawson Reed for helping us come up with a cover. He was the model fisherman who spent about an hour of valuable time out in the cold with a stringer of trout and a fishing rod. These students I got to meet made me realize the traditions I saw fifty years ago, continue today. And thanks too, to Angela Williamson, Director of Alumni Affairs, and Gwen Simmons, Associate Professor of Library Science at School of the Ozarks, for helping me so much and being so patient in making sure we found all the photos we needed.

If you know a student anywhere who is deserving of a college education, without the funds to pay for it, willing to work... put him or her in this picture at College of the Ozarks simply by contacting the administration office at Point Lookout, Missouri.

In the early days of School of the Ozarks High School, and its transition into a four year college, this man made a big difference as the President for many years. In all the time I spent at the School, I never heard a bad word spoken about Dr. Good. He was a beloved leader.

*My old roommate and good friend
Darrell Hamby just keeps on catching fish.*

My old roommate Jay Johnson, widely known across the Ozarks as Woody P. Snow, recently retired to write books and paint. Occasionally, the two of us get together to have a good time, just like the old days at S of O.

Other books by Larry Dablemont

- **The Front Bench Regulars**
  ...wit and wisdom from back home in the hills
- **Ain't No Such Animal**
  ...and other stories from the Ozark Hills
- **Ridge-Runner**
  ...from the Big Piney to the Battle of the Bulge
- **Dogs, Ducks, and Hat-Rack Bucks**
  ...short stories for the outdoorsman
- **Memories from a Misty Morning Marsh**
  ...a duck hunter's collection
- **The Greatest Wild Gobblers**
  ...lessons learned from old-timers and old toms
- **Rivers to Run**
  ...swift water, sycamores, and small-mouth bass

For more information write to:

Lightnin' Ridge Books
Box 22
Bolivar • MO 65613

lightninridge@windstream.net
417-777-5227